In Defense of Public Schools
In North America

John W. Friesen, Ph.D.
Virginia Lyons Friesen, Ph.D.

Detselig Enterprises Ltd.
Calgary, Alberta, Canada

In Defense of Public Schools in North America

Cataloging in Publication Information:

Friesen, John W.
  In defense of public schools in North America

  Includes bibliographical references.
  ISBN 1-55059-224-6

  1. Public schools – Canada. 2. Public schools – United States. 3.
Education – Canada. 4. Education – United States. I. Friesen,
Virginia Agnes Lyons II. Title.
LA412.F74   2001   371.01'0971   C2001-910901-6

Detselig Enterprises Ltd.
210, 1220 Kensington Road NW
Calgary, Alberta, Canada T2N 3P5

Phone: (403) 283-0900
Fax: (403) 283-6947
email: temeron@telusplanet.net
website: www.temerondetselig.com

Detselig Enterprises Ltd. recognizes the assistance from the Book
Publishing Industry Development Program (BPIDP) for its publishing
program.

ISBN 1-55059-224-6   Printed in Canada   SAN 115-0324

To Deborah Kae Zuercher Friesen,
Our favorite daughter-in-law

Contents

Introduction 11
  Is Criticism of Schools a Right? 12
  Public School Aims 14
  Still a Job To Do 16
  Enamor With Social Change 17

1 The Development of Public Education in North America . . .19
  Education in the United States 19
    First Nations' Education 19
    European Invasion 20
    Colonial America 21
    The Nineteenth Century 21
    Modern Times 22
    Recent Developments 22
    Towards the Future 24
  Education in Canada 24
    Lower Canada 25
    Upper Canada 27
    The Act Of Union 28
    The Maritime Provinces 29
    In the West 30
    Philosophy of Education 31
    Public Perceptions of Public Education 32

2 Public Schooling in the Last Half Century:
   A Miracle of Survival 35
    Two Metaphors 37
   Anti-Public School Campaigns: The 1950s 37
   The 1960s 39
    Summerhill 41
    The School Without Walls 43
    Community Schools 44
    Minority Concerns 46
   The 1970s 48
    Cooperative Learning 49
    Effective Schools 51
   The 1980s 52
    Quest for Change 54
   The 1990s 56

3 The Philosophical Whimsy of Public Education 59
  Identifying Basic Perspectives 60
  Traditionalism 61
    The Great Books Approach 63
    Updating Traditionalism 65
    The Spiritual Dimension 66
  Progressive Education 67
    Building a New Social Order 69
    The Canadian Connection 70
  Vocational Education 71
    One or Two Systems 72
    The Cult of Efficiency 72
    Science Rules 74
    Philosophically Unanchored in the 21st Century 75

4 Private and Parochial Schools: The Traditional Alternative 79
  Origins of Public Schooling 80
    The Roman Catholic Experience .81
    The Canadian Scene 82
    Alternative Schools in Canada 84
  Public Versus Private Schools 85
    Defending Private Schools 85
    Criticism of Private Schools 86
  Analysis 89
    The Equality Factor 90
    Need for Public Schools 94

5 Redesigning Public Education in America:
  The Business Approach 97
  The Quest for Diversity 98
    Philosophical Concerns 98
    Historical Roots 100
    Later Developments 102
    The Financial Factor 103
  The Voucher Plan 104
    The Alum Rock Experiment 106
    The California Family Choice Initiative 108
    Reviewing Vouchers 109
  Tuition Tax Credits 112
    Debating Tuition Tax Credits 113

Performance Contracting 115
   The Performance Contracting Plan 117
   Analysis 119
   The Continued Push 120

6 Home Schooling As Antithesis 123
   Why Home Schooling? 123
   The Data Bank of Home Schooling 124
   Home Schooling Claims 125
   State Requirements 126
   The Values Claim 126
   Analysis 128
   Two-Way Criticisms 128

7 Charter Schools: New Kid on the Block 131
   Defining Charter Schools 132
   Charter School Claims 134
   Criticisms 136
   Status of Teachers 138

8 Public Education For the 21st Century 141
   Multicultural Concerns 142
   Cultural Diversity in the United States 144
   Canadian Multiculturalism 145
   Schooling on the Frontline 147
   The Global Concern 149
   The Global Creed 150
   Five Steps to a Global Outlook .151
   Tolerance 152
   Understanding 152
   Acceptance 153
   Appreciation 154
   Affirmation 154

9 Improving Public Education 157
   Violence in Schools 159
   Towards a Solution 161
   Where to Now? 163

References 165

No other people ever demanded so much of education as have the Americans. None other was ever served as well by its schools and educators.

– Henry Steele Commager, American historian (1902-   )

About the Authors

John W. Friesen, Ph.D., D.Min., D.R.S., has been involved in public education in Canada and the United States for more than three decades. He is Professor in the Faculty of Education and the Faculty of Communication and Culture at the University of Calgary where he teaches courses in teacher training and Aboriginal education. He has taught secondary school in Kansas and holds an Alberta teaching certificate in secondary social studies. He is the author of more than thirty books including:

Profiles on Canadian Educators. (with Robert S. Patterson and John W. Chalmers). D.C. Heath, 1974;

Schools With A Purpose. Detselig, 1983;

Reforming the Schools – For Teachers. University Press of America, 1987;

Introduction to Teaching: A Socio-Cultural Approach (with Alice L. Boberg). Kendall/Hunt, 1990;

The Real/Riel Story: An Interpretive History of the Métis People of Canada. Borealis; 1996, and,

Aboriginal Spirituality and Biblical Theology: Closer Than You Think, Detselig, 2000.

Virginia Lyons Friesen, Ph.D., is a self-employed Early Childhood Education Specialist and holds a Certificate in Counselling from The Institute of Pastoral Counseling in Akron, Ohio. She has many years of teaching experience in early childhood education and has co-presented a number of papers at educational conferences. She is co-editor of *Grade Expectations:A Multicultural Handbook for Teachers,* published by the Alberta Teachers' Association in 1995.

Introduction

"Education for All: Will It Ever Happen?" was the slogan of the World Education Forum held in April, 2000, in Dakar, Senegal, but the one thousand national educational ministers from 180 countries attending the conference, had to go home disappointed. Ten years earlier, at the previous conference of the organization, world leaders had promised education for all by the year 2000. Now conference participants learned that this goal had not been reached. Today, more than 110 million children in the world do not have access to primary school, and another 150 million leave school before they have learned to read and write. These numbers can be added to the 872 million illiterate adults in the world (Rettig and Hynd, 2000).

While these dismal figures are being broadcast and the yearning for literacy continues, North Americans, by contrast, are busy dismantling their system of universal public education. Annually in Canada and the United States thousands of children are removed from public schools by their parents on the grounds the system is no longer delivering the goods. Private school enrollments are again rising, home schooling is burgeoning (House, 1988) and charter schools are being hailed as the innovative solution to the educational ills of the twenty-first century.

Generally speaking, the public has great faith in education. People demand education for their children and for themselves, so they set up public school systems and assign them the responsibility of opening their doors to any and all who can profit by attendance. They even tax themselves heavily year after year to pay the continually rising costs of education. As a result they expect their schools to accept responsibility for educating their children (Burrup, 1960). Unfortunately, as of late parents are withdrawing their children on grounds that school services can be offered more effectively elsewhere.

Despite its positive endorsement over past generations, public education seems always to be in a state of crisis. It is currently under fire by those who would prefer to replace it with other options, and this kind of trend will unfortunately wither away public education and eventually lead to further social inequities. It is just a bit illogical that public schooling has to face such duress since the record shows that over the past generations public schooling has maintained a pretty good record of proving literary skills to the body politick. Perhaps criticisms seem easy to render because schooling is a public enterprise and so it is everyone's right to judge what goes on in schools.

Ironically, most of the people who manage so succinctly to criticize public schools are also graduates of that institution. One wonders, where did they learn to formulate their concerns so articulately? And what makes them so angry that they have to bite the hand that intellectually fed them?

Is Criticism of Schools a Right?

Public schools have recently become the target of much criticism, much of it unwarranted. In Canada only 49 percent of those polled by Gallup in 1989 believed that their children were getting a better education than they did. This compares with 77 percent who felt that way in 1949 (Guppy and Davies, 1999). Despite this eroding sense of confidence, the truth is that public schools are necessary. Although alternatives should always remain the democratic right of parents and often serve a useful purpose, the fragmentation of a much needed institution like the public school has been overdone. It is time to retreat from the onslaught of condemning the very institution that can best prepare future generations for the much needed twenty-first century global perspective.

Critics of public education over the past half century have perpetually employed the term crisis, as though to imply that things have never been so bad before. It is true that many schools in both Canada and the United States are in need of evaluation, repair and updating. Other dismal realities include the fact that we have an aging population dependent upon fixed incomes, a shrinking corporate tax base to support schools, and a proliferation of litigation against schools (Baines et al., 1999). As a result many parents with available financial resources have withdrawn their children from public schools and have made alternative arrangements for them. Despite this disillusionment, year after year public schools continue to function and turn out graduates who take their various places in society both in business and industry as well as in the social realm. Many graduates even prepare themselves to return to school to serve as teachers.

To illustrate the ever recurring theme of "crisis in education" since the tempestuous 1960s, consider the following gems:

> To me the crucial aspect of our educational situation is this: We are at the threshold of a revolution in education, a revolution which will alter drastically every important aspect of education as a social institution and as a profession.

> Myron Lieberman, *The Future of Public Education*. 1960: 1-2.

> Throughout the length and breadth of our land public education is being debated as never before. Most of the discussion has to do with fundamental issues and some of it is well reasoned and pointed . . . all

of what is being said and written seems to indicate that our schools are indeed in a period of crisis.

James E. Frasier, *An Introduction to the Study of Education.* 1965: 8.

Anomalies appear in vast, accelerating numbers, and a "crisis state" exists. We are well aware of the need for a new ideological paradigm to help us come to grips with the problems of a highly interdependent and technologically advanced social order.

Richard Pratte, *Ideology & Education.* 1977: 113.

Despite limited resources, public schooling since about 1963 has presented a pattern of overall decline . . . for 18 years virtually every high school graduating class has been dumber than the preceding year's class.

Andrew Oldenquist, *Education 84/85.* 1984: 90.

The nation's public schools are in trouble. By almost every measure – the commitment and competency of teachers, student test scores, truancy and dropout rates, crimes of violence – the performance of our schools falls far short of expectations.

Josephy Murphy, *The Educational Reform Movement of the 1980s.* 1990: 3.

Our education system is no longer competitive with systems in the most advanced nations; schools are too costly to maintain in their present form; too much attention is placed on frivolous programs to the neglect of the basics; there is not enough discipline and respect for traditional values in the school; education system and personnel need to be made more accountable to the public; schools need to be more responsive to market forces . . .

Terry Wotherspoon, *The Sociology of Education in Canada.* 1998: 193.

Canada's public school system is struggling under the strain of funding cuts, labour strife and the needs of an increasingly diverse student body. The signs of stress abound . . . a growing number of Canadians are beginning to question whether or not the system can survive – and if so, how.

John Schofield, *Maclean's,* 2001: 22-23

Komisar (1992) notes that a favorite criticism of North American public schools is a comparison of student test scores with those of other developed nations. According to the results of international competitions, North American students do not always win. In a way this is like comparing amateurs against professionals, since North American youth are kept in school much longer than their international counterparts who turn their youth out to specialized jobs much earlier. As a result test scores reveal a difference in average levels of achievement in specialized fields which North American high school students have not delved into very deeply. Komisar suggests that instead of using test scores, critics ought to concentrate on the number of Nobel prizes won by any given country, the rate of patents applied for, or institutional rankings used in hiring. Test scores aren't everything.

It was more than one hundred and fifty years ago that Horace Mann (1796-1859) made the claim that a democratic educational system was the only vehicle by which literary equality could be assured for a people. He strongly opposed school segregation of any kind, fearing that a nation's economic and ethnic diversity could be split asunder unless a common school instilled shared values. Today we have proof for his concerns; studies show that children who attend poor schools do poorly, whether they come from lower or middle classes. Middle class children perform less well in schools where the majority of students come from lower socio-economic classes, and they should not have to attend them any more than children from lower socio-economic classes should have to. Evidence suggests that middle class children will not be hurt by economic integration so long as schools remain predominantly middle class. Children from lower social classes will do better if they are allowed to attend such schools (Kahlenberg, 2000).

Improving public schools will cost money, there is no doubt about it, but there are also other factors that affect academic success. Schools today have taken on a myriad of tasks additional to teaching literary skills. Classes are larger, teachers' salaries have not kept pace with the rising cost of living, and increased technology has added new costs to schooling and forced the perpetual retraining of teachers who might otherwise have put their time into more important tasks. Good schools, which usually happen to be at least middle class, feature better English, a more global outlook, increased parental input and a stable teaching staff. In the final analysis, an increased money supply will matter to improving schools, but the people who make up the school matter more.

Public School Aims

Public schools from the time of their origin were based on the notion that valued societal knowledge, which everyone had a right to acquire, could be stored and transmitted in a unique setting. Some social sectors even viewed schools as islands of knowledge and virtue in a sea of ignorance. Schools were made compulsory in order to provide a normal avenue to adulthood for everyone in the sense that they would have access to essential knowledge and skills which they would need as adults. Educators were charged with protecting children against abuse and ignorance and the state was assigned the responsibility of providing resources, setting standards, certifying teachers and approving curricula. The provision of resources implied that the state allocate public tax dollars for the operation of schools, and mandate the certification of teachers on both academic and ethical grounds.

To a certain extent early North American public schools were modelled on industrial structures, adopting the powerful and successful metaphor of industry in their curriculum as the course to be run. Such concepts as competition, schedules, themed courses, group instruction, specialization testing and certification quickly formed the basis of the school bureaucracy. As Henchley (1988:38) notes, essentially,

> schools were based on the separation of work as job, education as schooling, and leisure as entertainment. School was the transition between play (the unreal world) and work (the real world) and it was a preparation for life.

As a life-preparing institution, the public school has been charged with a multitude of citizen-related responsibilities such as teaching the skills needed for induction into a culture, as well as the forms of knowing which that culture affords. The public school should be conceived of as an agency that at least partially attempts to service society's need for a skilled work force. It is also a mechanism that aims to prepare youth to deal with various social, economic and political challenges they will face as adults. In fact, the public school may be considered the major vehicle by which all segments of society can advance socially and economically. While all of this is going on school personnel are expected to facilitate personal autonomy and self-actualization on the part of students (Lucas, 1984). Without a doubt, a democratic society committed to the proposition that educational opportunities must be provided for all youth, should perceive the public school as the best vehicle through which all of these goals can be realized (Richey, 1979).

To be fair, public schools cannot serve everyone, and alternative forms have their place, including private schools and even home schools. It is the present rate of fragmentation of the public system that is alarming, however, for if a great majority of North American children are suddenly being educated in alternative ways, there will be little basis on which to build a national base for a peoplehood. Misunderstandings and possible value conflict situations can much more easily erupt in a nation best depicted by a series of subcultures, stratified sectors and literacy ghettos.

Still a Job To Do

Despite making every attempt to ensure the fulfillment of expected goals, public attitudes toward public schools have often been harshly critical, and far from being taken for granted, schooling is more likely discussed today in language that discloses powerful emotional feelings at least as often as knowledge of facts. In hundreds of communities across the continent, citizens have taken sides for or against public education and many have simply responded to their concerns by opting for alternatives.

Gilbert and Robbins (1998: vii) suggest that the basis for reform to "salvage public education from the junkpile" is to inject student input as intelligent, fully vested partners in the vital debate on school improvement. It is their conviction that students as recipients of policy are well positioned to offer insight as to the potential impact of policy. These authors suggest that since students have to live with school policy on a day to day basis, they are best positioned to make suggestions about needed change. Following the contemporary slogan that "we're all equal here as far as privilege is concerned, but only some of us will have to take responsibility," Gilbert and Robbins promote the idea that educators who bypass student input miss the opportunity to create quality programs that will satisfy student needs. The assumption inherent in this argument is that students will know best what kinds of programs they will need since they will have the best crystal ball on future economic and technological developments. Forward-sounding as this proposal is, it fails to take cognizance of the fact that students are in school to learn, not to teach. If they have such far-sighted perceptions on educational reform, is it even necessary for them to attend school?

It is true that the public school needs to clean up its act in many respects; one of them, for example, being lack of respect for property shown by students resulting in increasing vandalism. School violence is also on the rise. These problems are being tackled, however, and remedies are becoming available. In the year 2000 the FBI released a report after examining 18 major school shooting incidents in the United States, targeting a systematic procedure for threat assessment and intervention, that should be used judicially by educators and mental health professionals faced with evaluating potential threatening situations within their communities. This approach offers hope, but this hope is overshadowed by the urgency of the need for liberalizing and bringing together of the people. A splintering of public education is not a feasible approach at this time and is not fruitful.

Enamor With Social Change

Social change is now an inevitable fact of life although people over the age of forty were probably raised to believe that society is a relatively stable entity. This perspective will have to be amended. It is safe to say that no major social institution has been more subject to pressure for change than the public school system. Basically every social institution will continue to be restructured over the next few decades whether we like it or not. Some changes will no doubt be made for the sake of change or to enhance economic markets. Others will be necessitated by ever shifting technologies or simply due to boredom with available offerings. As human beings come to believe that they can control the planet's ecosystem and perhaps even the solar system, their vision of their role in the universe, along with ideas of the good and beautiful will assume even more optimistic proportions of control, which will incite even greater change in most sectors.

The phenomenon of change rules, and this perspective has influenced a myriad of social adjustments. Unfortunately, institutional loyalty is on the way out. People do not frequent the same restaurants or the corner store because they like the owner or the inventory. They choose to direct their patronage to whoever sponsors the best show in town, offers the best bargain, or features the most titillating decor. These factors underscore an even greater need for public education. If public education has shortcomings, they must be addressed corporately by all sectors of the community. This tack will require a great deal of creative design and offer a greater degree of autonomy and flexibility in school management.

The public school district in Edmonton, Alberta, has met the challenge of change by incorporating parental choice within its ranks. In 1995, with student enrollments slipping, and things generally stagnant in the public system, public school superintendent Emery Dosdall helped bring new life to Edmonton's educational atmosphere with a radical plan. That city's public school district now offers its clientele nearly thirty different school choices within its ranks, several of which are private schools (Schofield, 2001: 25). Among the alternatives from which to select is a Hebrew school, several Aboriginal schools, a school for military cadets, and another for budding ballerinas. There are schools for dropouts and street kids, a sports school, a host of foreign language schools (from German to Ukrainian), and a science school. All schools receive the same funding and are responsible to the same management body. Each school has an advisory committee that seeks out public input, and the plan has worked. Over the last six years the academic achievement of the students has increased and the system has been invigorated (Nikiforuk, 2000).

An innovative plan to combat disillusionment with public education has been gradually devised in Australia (Gamage, 1996). In 1967 the Currie

Report recommended the establishment of an Independent School Authority to oversee the whole system, supplemented by input from local school councils at individual schools. The model was implemented in 1974. After twenty years of experience with this model it became evident that some schools were faring better than others in terms of academic achievement. As a result, a study was undertaken to determine the characteristics of the most effective schools with a hope of developing a workable format for others to follow. Based on the principle of maintaining a strong school culture, the sustaining characteristics of an effective school were found to be: (i) collaborative planning and collegial relationships; (ii) a sense of community; (iii) clear goals and high expectations commonly shared; and, (iv) order and discipline. A study to determine the satisfaction level of participants in decision-making reveals that 58.5 percent believed that there had been some improvement in the way schools were run and 37.7 percent felt that significant improvements had been made. None of the school council members polled indicated any adverse effects.

Those who choose to bail out of their responsibility to fix the schools may be sorely disappointed when they discover that the alternative institutions they have opted for will also have problems or deficiencies, but they will have reduced resources on which to draw in addressing problems. There are reasons why we need public education, and the most important is that the diversity which corporate input offers is the best solution to today's challenges and tomorrow's future. This goal cannot be attained through the auspices of a dismantled education system.

One

The Development of Public Education in North America

You can't expect a boy to be depraved until he has been to a good school
– Saki (H. H. Munro) in *A Baker's Dozen.* (Cohen and Cohen, 1960: 303)

The basic premise on which critics of the public school system offer their complaints is that the public school is a servant of the people. This makes everyone an authority on education because the public "owns" the school and everyone once went to school. Historically things were not always so, for the concept of a "public" school actually originated as an institution designed exclusively for the elite of the nation, at least in Europe. In medieval times, such schools as Winchester, Eton and Elster were founded to train a priestly elite, but as these schools expanded they gradually transformed to train a political elite. Still later, they targeted the training of a managerial elite with a bias more towards commerce than industry. Clients of the schools paid elaborate fees in order to guarantee that their children would be able to qualify for lucrative positions among the nation's leadership (Musgrave, 1965). Following this model, the English grammar school imitated Winchester and Eton to some extent, stressing a sense of duty as virtuous and placing great emphasis on the mastery of literary skills. It was expected that students would use their abilities well and they would be examined according to their academic success.

Education in the United States

First Nations' Education

Long before the first Europeans landed on North American shores, the First Nations had in place an effective educational system that had guaranteed them cultural maintenance for centuries. Although the system was more informal than formal, except in the southwest United States (Friesen, 1993a), elements of the latter also prevailed, particularly in the form of religious sodalities which apprenticed youth in the rudiments of spirituality, medicinal knowledge and ceremonial life. Generally speaking, the education of the young was in the hands of grandparents and elders; the former taught by observation and modelling and the latter by storytelling and ceremony. Indian legends were frequently utilized as curriculum content by elders and although many of them were related for amusement or entertainment, there were also sacred legends that were shared only at certain times and places. These stories described the origins of natural phenomena, prescribed appropriate moral behavior for both boys and girls, and embued spiritual truths on which the foundations of the very culture were sustained (Friesen, 1997).

European Invasion

Sadly, when Indian communities were invaded by Europeans some five hundred years ago, many of the old ways were lost through deliberate destruction by the invaders. Since the newcomers came primarily to conquer and plunder they had little patience for learning about Indigenous ways. Besides, since Aboriginal lifestyles and beliefs were radically different than those of the invaders, they were quickly labelled "heathen" and every effort was made to disband the Indigenous Peoples of their belief systems. "Christianize, educate and civilize" was the slogan of many missionaries who followed the explorers to the new land, and once here they wasted no time in building churches and schools aimed at squelching Indian ways. Most hated of these institutions were residential or boarding schools where Indian youth were told that the ways of their grandfathers were evil and must be screened out. The result was that many Aboriginal youth grew up ashamed of being Native and developed low self-esteem which contributed to personally devastating habits such as substance abuse (Friesen, 2000: 109).

When the Puritans set foot on the "stern and rockbound coast" of what is now Massachusetts, they were firmly committed to a fundamentalist religious lifestyle and devised ingenious ways of perpetuating this orientation among their children. They were a deeply religious people who considered salvation the fundamental purpose of life and the primary purpose of schooling. Since children were considered spiritually depraved by the Puritans they believed that children needed to learn to read in order to be able to interpret the Scriptures. This perspective brought about a "public system" of education in the early American colonies committed to a mastery of the 3 R's, so that pupils would be able to read the Bible and thus better prepare themselves for eternity. According to the record, the founding of the Plymouth Colony at Jamestown marked the beginning of public education in America (Bayles and Hood, 1966).

Elite Latin grammar schools were popular in America between the years 1635 and 1750 when they were replaced by more democratic schools promoted by Benjamin Franklin. The curriculum of these schools was more practical, co-educational, and somewhat more relevant to the value system of the American middle class. During the colonial period generally, however, American schools were dominated by theological, social and political orthodoxies. Schools reflected British culture in that education was aristocratic and private.

Colonial America

The development of schooling in colonial America occurred with the greatest speed in the north with the colonies of Massachusetts and Connecticut leading the way. The motivation to establish schools was religious since the early colonists emigrated on religious grounds with an intense desire to transmit their beliefs to the next generation via formal instruction. The middle colonies were more reluctant to adopt all-out public educational institutions, because most colonists felt that parochial schools provided sufficient schooling for children of upper-class families. This attitude deterred the development of public schools. The plantation-saturated south was not interested in public schooling since a free and accessible system might interfere with their well-oiled class system of planters, working classes and slaves. In fact, between 1770 and 1800 it could be said that interest in education gradually declined in America due to the challenge emanating from increased immigration and the effects of the Industrial Revolution.

The Nineteenth Century

By the middle of the nineteenth century a quickening of interest in schools became evident as several states motivated the development of a state system of free public schools. Subsequently, the new public schools began to reflect a more open and democratic stance. Public education was free and more practical subjects were introduced into the curriculum. Horace Mann is credited with the title of "Father of Public Education in America" and the moving force in the Massachusetts legislature that enacted statutes establishing a state board of education and compulsory school attendance. The full public identity of the public school was realized in 1872 when the Michigan Supreme Court ruled that communities could raise money for school operations through taxation. After that, tax-supported schools substantially enrolled all school-aged children in America, regardless of race, ethnicity, religion or socio-economic status. Much of the philosophy of education advanced in the early days of these schools originated in the McGuffy

Readers first used in the State of Ohio and then published and used widely across the country.

Modern Times

As the twentieth century emerged, the American federal government began to assume a more active role in public education. Kindergartens were developed in public schools and the American high school was recognized as an entity in its own right. Social, economic and political forces were changing rapidly, forcing national leaders to try to keep abreast of a growing complexity of business and industrial life. In 1918 the National Education Association gained attention with the formulation of the Seven Cardinal Principles of Education: health, fundamental processes, worthy home membership, vocation, citizenship, worthy use of leisure time and ethical behavior. After the two World Wars extra attention was given to education when it was realized that members of the armed forces were mentally and/or physically unfit for military service. This fact encouraged the realization that education was in reality the frontline for national defense.

As the twentieth century rumbled on there were indications of significant changes on the philosophic horizon for American schools, particularly with the advent of such trends as progressive education advocated by John Dewey, William Heard Kilpatrick, Boyd Bode and George Sylvester Counts, who believed that schooling should be child-centred, democratic and relevant. The new theme was "learning by doing," based on the assumption that students' interest should be considered more important than formal subject matter. School content should be "meaningful" to students and individuality and self-expression should be prized. Dewey's ideas were followed up at the high school level by James B. Conant, former president of Harvard University and United States Ambassador to the Federal Republic of West Germany. In 1948, Conant advocated the development of high schools dedicated to the strengthening of science and language courses plus a varied curriculum with higher standards. Forty years later, under President George Bush, state governors agreed on six, and later under President Bill Clinton, eight national goals identified by Conant. A further practicality in education after Conant was introduced by Harvard educator, Jerome S. Bruner who promoted the idea that any subject could be taught to any child at any age, provided the material was presented in a logical and sequential manner.

Recent Developments

Education in the United States survived the turbid 1960s with its advocacy of open or "free" education and gained a new political status in 1979 when President Jimmy Carter announced that the Department of Education would be represented on its own in the cabinet. President Ronald Reagan tried to reverse this decision when he came to power, but his Education Secretary appointed the National Commission on Excellence in Education to prepare a report that shook the nation when it was published in 1983. Entitled *The Nation at Risk,* the report targeted the theme of mediocrity in the nation's schools by citing statistics showing that American students ranked 7 out of 19 on international tests of achievement. As efforts to implement the recommendations of the report got underway, a new wave of reform struck the educational landscape – parental choice in schooling. Polls in America now suggest that 60 percent of public schools favor school choice. The Republican Congress elected in 1994 decided that the institutionalization of school choice would force the closure of inefficient schools and leave only better schools on the horizon (Parker and Parker, 1995). Opponents of the idea believe that school choice will destroy public schools as we know them because of its contributing nature towards fragmentation.

Educational choice is based on a set of assumptions that generally challenge public education as we know it. Proponents of the idea denigrate the notion of a school system that responds to a democratically elected and bureaucratically managed hierarchical system, and instead propose a highly fragmented and decentralized system that responds directly to parental and student concerns. Curriculum and pedagogy are not directed from a centralized authority, but are set by individual schools in response to consumer desires. Accountability is based on family choice, not on the democratic process.

The concept of school choice has been amply studied (Froese-Germain, 1998), and the findings clearly indicate that increasing educational choice serves to increase separation of students by race, social class and cultural background. There is no systematic evidence that competitive school choice environments improve student learning. We do, however, know a lot about people who opt for school choice. Usually they are more affluent, have higher levels of education, and are quite heavily involved in their children's education (Witte and Thorn, 1996). Because of these factors, school choice tends to play to certain schools, such as charter schools, which manage to "cream off" the best students and thus impact negatively on local public schools who are left with fewer students who are higher-risk and with higher cost (McEwan and Carnoy, 2000). Enhancing school choice within a public school system, like the Edmonton School Board did, gives authenticity to the concept instead of making alternatives available to only a specific sector of the community.

Stated positively, there is advantage in keeping students of different backgrounds and abilities together. Willie (2000) points out that both Black and White students have high achievement scores in multicultural school settings (although not as high as in racially isolated White settings), but Black students tend to have higher achievement scores in multicultural schools compared with racially isolated Black settings. On this basis strong recommendations can be made for mixed student bodies in more schools. On a parallel note, for those who may wish to counter this conclusion, it is noteworthy to observe that desegregation can proceed effectively in communities where other institutions remain segregated. Benveniste and McEwan (2000) discovered that multigrade schools can have the same effect in which or where students mixed in age and ability can be a cost-effective means of raising student achievement and expand access in communities that could not otherwise afford it.

Towards the Future

As the twenty-first century emerges there is concern that public schooling, despite its struggles to persist, will effectively be dismantled. Whitty et al. (1998) point out that parental choice, school autonomy and shared decision-making are among the most popular school reform ideas for the twenty-first century. Logically, if there is to be parental choice, there must be alternatives from which to choose. If the alternatives available within a public system are deemed to be inadequate by choice-seekers, the movement towards further fragmentation may continue to gain momentum. In so far as school autonomy is concerned, if developments in Illinois are any indication, educators could be in for some interesting times. The Illinois legislature recently passed a bill expanding state control with initial inauguration to be in Chicago. The legislation requires Chicago schools to produce an annual report on student performance, meet various prespecified, state-set targets and implement particular categorical programs. Local school councils are to be set up with power to hire or fire school principals, set budgetary priorities, and establish curriculum themes (Whitty et al., 1998). Since local councils are made up of parents and community representatives the move should go a long ways towards guaranteeing parental input and perhaps reduce the degree of dissatisfaction with the way public schools are run.

Education in Canada

Schooling in Canada inspired by European roots may be traced back as early as 1640 when a young, would-be educator from France, Sister Marguerite Bourgeoys, following a vision, migrated to New France to teach religion. Targets of her mission included First Nations, children of the fur traders and settlers, and new brides, namely women who emigrated to the new world in quest of marriage partners and a new, more adventurous lifestyle. Bourgeoys had four educational aims in mind: religious training (Roman Catholic), social graces (including consideration of others and courtesy), the 3 R's, and house-wifely skills. In addition to her task as a teacher in the wilderness, after struggling for a long time to obtain her bishop's approval, Bourgeoys succeeded in establishing the Ursulines, the first uncloistered Order of Sisters in the Roman Catholic Church. The efforts of the Ursulines in providing primary education were complemented by the Sisters of Hôtel Dieu and the Sisters of the Congrégation de Notre Dame. The Jesuits and the Oblates worked at the secondary level, establishing their first college in Quebec.

During the seventeenth to nineteenth centuries the few Canadian schools established to provide primary education for children did so with great commitment to the cause. Few graduates of these schools went on to attend secondary schools or high schools as we know them today. Instead, most elementary graduates went on to work on farms or in factories or prepared themselves to become skilled tradesmen and tradeswomen through the process of apprenticeship. Secondary schools did not appear in full force in Canada until the late 1800s or early 1900s when they adopted curricula with greater breadth and became known as institutions to prepare youth for university entrance. The new curricula had four specific emphases: commercial, technical, agricultural, physical sciences and fine arts (Gue, 1985).

The British North America Act of 1867 (BNA Act) united the Province of Canada (Upper and Lower Canada), New Brunswick and Nova Scotia into four provinces – Quebec, Ontario, New Brunswick and Nova Scotia, under a federal form of government. Five other provinces joined confederation later including Manitoba in 1870, British Columbia in 1871, Prince Edward Island in 1873, and Alberta and Saskatchewan, which were formed and added in 1905. Newfoundland was the newest province to join in 1949. Each province formed its own government with specific legislative and executive powers including rights pertaining to education.

Lower Canada

Specific educational developments in Lower Canada (now Quebec) evolved slowly. Audet (1970a) suggests that this evolution occurred in three specific stages: the *first* stage, 1760-1789, is best described as a period of private education. During the period of French domination and following the Treaty of 1763 by which Canada became a British colony, there were few schools in Lower Canada. The first French school system, if it may be called such, was initiated by the Roman Catholic Church and operated without government assistance. Any attempts to develop alternative forms of schooling were strongly opposed by Roman Catholic clergy.

The *second* stage of education in Lower Canada occurred between the years 1790 to 1801 highlighted by attempts to establish public school systems. By 1790 the efforts of the Roman Catholic clergy had encouraged the development of forty educational institutions in Lower Canada accompanied by a growth in immigrant population from 75 000 to 160 000. The Protestant population had an least seventeen schools in operation for 10 000 inhabitants. Despite these efforts most of the population was illiterate.

The *third* stage of education in Lower Canada was initiated in 1801 when the British colonial government made overtures towards state control by passing "an Act for the Establishment of Free Schools and the Advancement of Learning in this province." Essentially the act provided for the establishment of free common schools when a majority of citizens in an area petitioned for a school and declared themselves willing to pay for its operation. Naturally, the Roman Catholic Church opposed the act, fearing that it would give the Church of England (Anglican Church) a new role in education. Very few free common schools were established as a result of this act.

In 1829 the legislature of Lower Canada tried again, this time by establishing a new central education authority accompanied by a new legislative act pertaining to schooling. This act provided that trustees could be elected by the members of a community to form a local school authority and the government would provide a grant for any initiated school of twenty or more pupils. This act eventually encouraged the establishment of large numbers of non-Catholic schools in Lower Canada.

The architect for Lower Canada's common school system was also their first school superintendent, Jean-Baptiste Meilleur. Meilleur relied heavily on the power of his pen to initiate change and establish a uniform school system, as evidenced in his annual reports, his circulars to school commissioners and inspectors, his drafts of school laws and his private correspondence. Meilleur was greatly influenced by developments in the New England States where he witnessed flourishing elementary and secondary schools supported by state taxation and taught by trained and inspected teachers. When public schools were only weakly supported in Lower Canada, Meilleur emulated the Joseph Lancaster system whereby older students were used as monitors to drill younger children in the fundamentals. Meilleur also introduced the idea of school gardens as a means of teaching agricultural methods to students who he believed would grow up to be farmers anyway. He advocated that teachers "board around" by staying with a different family each month so they could offer additional instruction to local families during evenings. So anxious was he to establish universal schooling opportunities that he opposed fixed salaries for teachers, arguing that wages should reflect local socio-economic circumstances in order not to impose an undue financial burden on the community.

Upper Canada

Upper Canada was established in 1791 when the Constitutional Act separated this part of the colony from Lower Canada. Grammar schools were established by the Grammar School Act in 1807 and elementary schools by the Common School Act of 1816. In 1823 the colonial government passed another piece of legislation to set up a central board of education whose members were appointed with powers prescribed by government. The central board was assigned powers to select textbooks, set up courses of study and prescribe teacher qualification.

English influence on Upper Canadian education may be earmarked by the rise to power of the colony's first Lieutenant-Governor, John Graves Simcoe. Educated in Britain's elite culture, Simcoe conceived of education as a right of the very few who would eventually become the nation's leaders. For the rest, Simcoe held that "such education as may be necessary for people in the lower degrees of life . . . may at present be provided for them by their connections and relations" (Wilson, 1970: 193). The curriculum of the elite schools would concentrate on the classics and a university would be built for their students' later development and educational enrichment. Simcoe did achieve government support for two of his grammar schools and after he left Upper Canada the colony's legislation petitioned King George III for a land grant to provide for a grammar school in every district and a university in the colony capital. Eventually the grammar schools became known as district schools but since the schools charged very high tuition, only children of the well-to-do could afford to attend. Teachers were religiously-affiliated, usually with the Church of England even though that denomination was not officially designated as the established church by the Constitutional Act of 1791.

In 1815 Anglican Bishop John Strachan was appointed to the Executive Council of Upper Canada and soon thereafter submitted a plan for common school education to the council. Strachan called for the creation of a system of common schools that would provide basic education to all children in the province. Strachan also envisaged the establishment of district grammar schools which were designed mostly for the elite. He arranged that tuition free vouchers would be made available to children of poorer families so that ten students from these families could attend each of the eight grammar schools that were set up. Most of the fundamental principles of the Common School Act of 1816 could be attributed to Strachan's efforts.

In 1839, Lord Durham (whose name was John George Lambton), Earl of Durham, and later Lord High Commissioner, issued a report on education recommending that schools be set up in all regions of Upper Canada. The report made note of the fact that many areas of the province were completely without schools and those that existed were of very inferior character. A committee headed by the president of the University of Toronto was established to investigate Durham's charges, and soon concluded that only 55-60 percent of school-aged children were attending school. Instead of instant reform, however, this condition prevailed until after the Act of Union was consummated.

The Act of Union

The situation in Upper and Lower Canada was affected by the Act of Union of 1841 which decreed that the two Canadas would become one united colony. In terms of schooling, the Act gave municipal councils the right to build public schools and levy taxes to fund them. It also gave boards of education the authority to levy taxes to build schools. Religious minorities were also given authority to withdraw from common school systems and establish their own schools with their own school boards (Cheal et al., 1962).

In 1846 all previous school legislation was repealed and a new Education Act was passed. Although the act retained many of the previously established provisions it was informally known as the great charter of education for the Province of Quebec. There were to be one or more schools set up in each municipality administered by elected trustees who were independent of municipal councils. Dissentient (dissenting) schools were to be placed under the supervision of three trustees, and the government offered grants to run the schools provided they operated for at least eight months of the year. By the time of Confederation, a fairly definite pattern of schooling had been established; the colonial government administered the school system but left severe gaps in terms of providing an equitous system.

Upper Canada benefited greatly from the dedicated efforts of Egerton Ryerson, sometimes called the "Father of English-speaking Canadian education." Ryerson was well known in Upper Canada as a preacher, writer, editor and negotiator. He began his educational career as principal of the Methodist Academy in Upper Canada in 1842 and two years later became Superintendent of Education for the province. Ryerson was of the conviction that education should be compulsory, universal, practical, Christian (but nonsectarian), and free. When the Upper Canada legislature passed the Common School Act in 1846 it incorporated most of Ryerson's ideas by centralizing most aspects of the provincial system under Ryerson's control. In 1850 when his concerns had been met Ryerson proposed a significant decentralization by giving trustee boards power to raise necessary taxes.

Ryerson believed that universal elementary education would decrease crime and poverty, and increase efficiency, promote happiness and yield compliance to the rule of the people, but he did not expect it to act as a levelling force in society. Not particularly given to egalitarian ideas, Ryerson hoped education would fit "children for their place in the social hierarchy"

(McNeill, 1974: 134). By the time of his retirement in 1876 Ryerson could boast that Ontario (formerly Upper Canada), had in operation an extensive, coordinated public school system which served the general needs of the people of that province.

The Maritime Provinces

During the eighteenth century regional differences flourished in Canada and the largest proportion of population was in the east. While Upper and Lower Canada were busy establishing state systems of education, Britain's colonies on the Atlantic coast were addressing the challenge in quite different ways. The governments of the Atlantic provinces, New Brunswick, Nova Scotia and Prince Edward Island were generally reluctant to get involved in the educational affairs of their jurisdictions, and progress that was made towards any form of public education was undertaken by religious denominations. Nova Scotia, strongly influenced by Anglican-Loyalist concerns, and the tireless efforts of one Rev. Charles Inglis, initiated a common school movement in 1787. Then, in 1818, a Scottish Presbyterian clergyman, Thomas McCulloch, began Pictou Academy, and devoted his school to nonsectarian, democratic and liberal education. By 1825, Nova Scotia had 217 such schools in operation. A contemporary of Thomas McCulloch in Newfoundland, Edward Feild, set up an Anglican school system in that province in 1844. This action opened the door for an unusual marriage between religion and education that spawned the formation of further denominational school districts, a situation that earmarked Newfoundland's approach as unique. On April 29, 1874 the Newfoundland legislature gave formal approval to the concept of denominational school systems (Netten, 1974).

Also subject to Loyalist influence, New Brunswick had a number of different schools in operation by 1793, some of them sponsored by the Society for the Propagation of the Gospel and the National Society. The latter sponsored monitorial schools known as Madras schools which were cheap to run and strong on discipline. In 1805 the foundation for secondary education was laid via the "Act for Encouraging and Extending Literature in the Province." In 1852 legislation was passed to install the first superintendent of education in New Brunswick, and in 1861 the Provincial Board of Education took over control of public education in the Province.

Efforts to provide public education of any kind were meagre in Prince Edward Island during the first half of its existence as a province, but by the end of the eighteenth century this was all to change. In Scottish settlements, both Protestant and Roman Catholic schools were in operation, and the latter also appeared in Acadian settlements. In 1834 Prince Edward Island formalized a central authority for their schools and the control of the grammar schools in 1861.

In the West

Most of the events that transpired in the Canadian west during the nineteenth century had to do with the discovery of gold, the diminishing fur trade and the gradual settlement of the prairies. The first schools built in the west were the result of the missionary efforts of both Roman Catholic and Protestant missionaries. Both denominations received grants from the Hudson's Bay Company as encouragement for providing schools for children of the company's employees. The first school system in the west occurred when the government of the new united colony in British Columbia passed the Common School Ordinance of 1869. Manitoba became a province in 1870, largely due to the efforts of Louis Riel, and the new government quickly validated the existence of denominational schools. The following year the province's Initial Education Act was formulated which created a dual educational system of Protestant (now public) and Separate or Roman Catholic schools. Alberta and Saskatchewan did not emerge as provinces until 1905 when their separate identities were carved out of the North West Territories. Public and separate (Protestant or Roman Catholic) school systems were established in those provinces shortly thereafter.

One of the most significant happenings in western Canadian education occurred in 1890 when the Manitoba Government decided to initiate a single non-sectarian school system, patterned after the British Columbia model. Roman Catholic leaders, who up till that time had been operating a denominational system, opposed the move quoting the British North America Act which guaranteed minority rights in education. The resultant dispute raged for six years and came to a compromise by the Laurier-Greenway Agreement in 1897 which stipulated a single, public non-denominational school system for Manitoba. The die was cast, and by a stroke of the pen all denominational schools were suddenly non-legal entities. It was then decreed that minority rights in education would be preserved by the following arrangement; if numbers warranted, in any school district, religious minorities would be given permission to offer religious instruction in public schools for a half-hour at the end of each school day. It was agreed that a proportion of Roman Catholic teachers would be employed by the public system depending on the number of Roman Catholic children enrolled. Finally, the Laurier-Greenway Agreement specified that

> when ten of the pupils in any school speak the French language, or any language other than English as their native language, the teaching of

such pupils shall be conducted in French or such language, and English upon the bilingual. (Johnson, 1968: 95)

Immigration to the Canadian west exploded under the leadership of Clifford Sifton who became Minister of the Interior in 1896. Between 1896 and 1912 immigration totalled over 2 500 000. In 1913, the peak year, 400 870 people entered Canada. Most of the schools in the west during this time operated according to the Territorial Ordinances of 1885-1886 and were supervised by David J. Goggin who was superintendent. In 1905 when the two new provinces were launched, Alberta had 551 schools and Saskatchewan had 206. By 1944 both provinces had developed larger school districts as a means of bringing some element of standardization to their systems. While the federal government never formed a central office of education, assistance was given to the provinces by such means as technical and vocational assistance, educational broadcasting and the National Film Board.

Philosophy of Education

It is difficult to pinpoint the fundamental qualities of Canadian education because the early pioneers represented a variety of national backgrounds and customs which resulted in a very mixed educational composition. One of the more obvious themes to echo throughout Canada's early schools was religion, since all early schools were founded on a Christian foundation. The partisan systems, Public and Separate, which operate today in several provinces are a living testimony to the nature of Canadian society in the seventeenth and eighteenth centuries. Closely related to the factor of religion is the reality of the two major backgrounds of the "founding nations," namely English and French. It is only within the last half of the twentieth century that any notions of multiculturalism have arisen.

When the philosophy of progressive education invaded American schools, there were Canadians who read their works and were influenced by them. In Nova Scotia, Loren DeWolfe followed John Dewey on the notion that the role of experience instead of curriculum content in the educational process should be primary. As Director of Rural Science for the province, he developed an "experience-centred" curriculum for Nova Scotia's schools, stressing that personal experience should be considered the sum total of education. Meanwhile, his contemporary in Alberta, Hubert C. Newland, Supervisor of Schools for the province, popularized three specific progressive principles: *first*, growth is dependent, not upon what is done for students, but what students do for themselves; *second*, developmental growth is not segmental, but total; and *third*, mental development takes place when efforts to reach a goal are evaluated (Patterson, 1974). Although Alberta took more kindly to the language of progressive education than most other provinces, its fundamentals were never really implemented in the province's schools.

Public Perceptions of Public Education

Dissatisfaction with public education today seems to represent an entirely different cerebral environment than has previously been the case. Parents who pick on schools do so from the perspective of having attained a higher level of achievement in literacy; people in North America are simply much better educated today than they have ever been before. Of course the publicly-funded school system is to be thanked for this, since most North Americans attain a grade twelve diploma these days. In addition, in Canada and the United States, post-secondary education now reaches over forty percent of all those who begin school and that percentage is rising (Winchester, 2000). The result is a highly educated, cultured and literate population, and the people know what they want. Rather than spending time on their knees giving thanks for such a wonderfully effective institution, many are either planning ways to improve the institution that has brought them thus far, or avoiding it altogether.

As already indicated, an educated body politick is well aware that they are paying for public schools and they want a say it its operation. People are no longer prepared to quietly acquiesce to the practice of unwittingly shelling out tax dollars without being able to offer input. This challenge now has to be faced by politicians who have long been used to making decisions and spending locally-raised monies in faraway places like provincial, state and federal capitals. Even home schoolers are demanding their just portion of school tax dollars in order to establish intimate learning groups involving parents or parent-hired teachers.

In addition to having to play to a more enlightened constituency, public schooling also faces an entirely different student body. In traditional times, students were expected to be passive learners, virtual consumers of the wisdom marketed by educational authorities. Individual inquiry was not encouraged and most subject matter was presented in a take-it-or-leave-it fashion. Small wonder that Albert Einstein had to drop out of school in order to invent the theory of relativity. Today, students are not only encouraged to engage in inquiry and analysis but they are expected to find intrinsic value in learning.

Historically, public schools in larger centers existed in relative isolation from the community and criticisms of the institution were scarce. In a sense urban schools were once ideal communities set apart from the rest of society. Not everyone was of the conviction that what went on in school was necessarily relevant to life in "the real world." An extreme example of abuse in this context were Indian residential or boarding schools which operated in both the United States and Canada. Children were taken from their families and shunted off to a distant location to learn an entirely different language, religion, and form of social structure. This form of schooling possibly represented one of the widest gaps between school and life ever witnessed on this continent. Closer to home, there were many rural communities who saw compulsory education as an infringement on their agricultural needs. Older students were often kept at home during spring seeding time as well as during harvest because their energies were perceived to be better directed towards enhancing the food supply than memorizing multiplication tables.

Keeping up to date on school developments is the business of the United States Office of Education in Washington DC. There its personnel collect and publish statistics on education, provide national leadership in the area, and engage in research. A different situation prevails in Canada where there is no national office of education. By order of the constitution of the country, education is under the sole jurisdiction of each of the ten provinces. The Canadian Education Association (CEA), which is located in Toronto substitutes to some extent for a national office of education by sponsoring conferences, keeping noting and drawing statistics, and commissioning research on educational developments in each of the provinces and territories. The CEA has thirty-five members of which twelve positions are reserved for provincial and territorial ministries of education and in order to respect the two official languages, at least eight of the members much be English-speaking and eight must be French-speaking. Board members are expected to promote the broader interest of education in Canada rather than the particular interests of the areas which they individually represent. Publications of the CEA provide a national perspective on educational developments in the various regions of the nation. It would do critics a lot of good if they first consulted these agencies of information before they loose their often unsubstantiated criticisms of public schools.

Two

Public Schooling in the Last Half Century:
A Miracle of Survival

Although the phenomenon of public education is often taken for granted only two centuries ago the idea of a "common school" was a much debated topic in North America. Apple (2000) suggests that public schools from the beginning were and still represent a victory for the common people. Public schools are a boon for the majority of people who would otherwise be denied access to advancement and valued cultural capital in a stratified society. It was only in the middle of the nineteenth century that the championing efforts of Horace Mann and Henry Barnard for public schooling resulted in the acceptance of the concept. The emerging consensus was that public schools should be built and charged with providing the basic knowledge and skills essential to enable students of diverse backgrounds to assume the responsibilities of citizenship. As Mann stated in his essay of 1848, "Means and Objects of Common School Education" (Foy, 1968: 19-20):

> We want a generation of men above deciding great and eternal principles, upon narrow and selfish grounds. Our advanced state of civilization has evolved many complicated questions respecting social duties. We want a generation of men capable of taking up these complex questions, and of turning all sides of them towards the sun, and of examining them by the white light of reason, and not under the false colors which sophistry may throw upon them. We want no men who will change, like the vanes of our steeples, with the course of the popular wind.

For the next several generations Mann's recipe for success was debated and basically perpetuated despite becoming the target of a myriad of philosophical onslaughts manipulated by both liberals and conservatives. The conservative faction was championed by Robert Maynard Hutchins (1943), then Chancellor of the University of Chicago, aided by a colleague, Mortimer Adler. Hutchins observed that public schools were in a state of mediocrity, having yielded to the visceral impulse to give up anything intellectual in the curriculum. His diagnosis was supported by Albert Lynd, Arthur Bestor, Jr., and Admiral Hyman Rickover, who promoted the Jeffersonian principle that anything short of science, language, mathematics and history was tantamount to turning the schools over to illiterates. John Dewey's progressivism was attacked on the basis that it lacked academic rigor and relied too much on the insights of inexperienced children for curriculum building.

Naturally, the progressivists fought back, particularly William Heard Kilpatrick, a loyal follower of Dewey, who more than any other individual popularized the teachings of his mentor. He argued that dry history, stale mathematics, sterile science and useless grammar kept youngsters from learning the essential meaning of any subject matter which they needed to know in order to be able to cope in an ever changing environment. Kilpatrick blamed the alleged mediocrity in schools on proponents of the old philosophies who held fast to the authoritarianism of old knowledge, past science, past religion and past ethics. The debate raged, and when the dust had cleared, there was something in it for everyone, but nobody won. The schools adopted something of each view which resulted in a strange admixture of holding to fundamentalistic teachings and progressive methods of dealing with subject matter. New subjects did infiltrate the curriculum, much to the chagrin of the traditionalists. The new subjects included driver education, education for socialization, preparation for college and even sex education (Mehl, 1963).

By the beginning of the 20th century, public schooling had become an established institution. Now the challenge was to determine how best to govern schools and set them on the right track philosophically. Some educational leaders opted for G. Stanley Hall's theory of genetic psychology while others followed the lead of pragmatic thinkers like John Dewey, William James and Charles Saunders Pierce. Proponents of Hall's ideas adopted the specific objectivist theories of Edward L. Thorndike and B. F. Skinner's theory of operant conditioning. Philosophical arguments favoring one or the other of these theories raged, interrupted only by the two World Wars after which a kind of educational lull set in.

By the 1960s, reform movements again appeared on the horizon. The first announcement of the new campaign championed the slogan that schooling was in a state of crisis! Schools became the focus for planners who sought vast social and economic changes to please politicians. Essentially politicians who envisaged the formation of national cohesion via education were joined by ordinary citizens who wanted more of the good life than society had to offer. Most of these lobbyists were agreed that schools had the power to generate new levels of modernization and to respond to the needs of an industrial society, but they were not the ones to draw the attention of the public media. It was the doomsayers, those disillusioned with the potential of schooling who expressed their unhappiness with the institution in radical ways by posing radical solutions. A primary objection to schooling was that schools were clearly imperfect instruments as social levellers. A few obstreperous individuals even questioned whether the good life should be defined in terms of more of the same (Adams, 1972).

Two Metaphors

In retrospect it is probably fair to say that for at least the first half of the 20th century, two metaphors dominated the public's thinking about schools and about learning, teaching and teacher education. The *first* metaphor was that schools should function like factories and churn out needed products for a consuming society. As a result schools should be managed by tight business-like management techniques. The *second* metaphor portrayed schooling as a craft in which work was routine. In both scenarios workers were to do what supervisors told them to do and new practitioners simply followed the practices of their more experienced masters (Myers and Simpson, 1998).

The notion that schools were factories probably caught the public eye at the beginning of the 20th century because the concept was already deeply embedded in industrialization in the United States. It is quite possible that the metaphor never did fit what was going on in schools (with a few exceptions, of course), but it was a quick and easy format by which to judge the end result. This perspective also lent credence to the notion that schools should be operated by business-oriented individuals who would be willing to provide the public with the most for their money. The impact on school administration was to design the control format for schools on a business model with a hierarchy of accountants and managers. In any large school featuring several layers of supervisors, students were lucky even to meet the principal before the day of their graduation.

Another variation of the factory model was the teaching-as-craft concept which weighed more heavily on the teacher's role. It was seen as the teacher's primary responsibility to hone each child towards a prescribed objective – master the 3 R's and prepare for the job pool. Educators soon realized the deficiency with this approach in that teaching requires much more than craft knowledge and it is anything but routine.

Teachers are daily confronted with unforeseen challenges; in fact, their duties assume several quite distinct obligations which require them to be knowledgeable, investigative, decision-making, executive managers. Human beings (both students and teachers) do not function in assembly-line fashion, and the best trained craftsmen simply cannot foresee how individuals other than themselves may perceive things.

Anti-Public School Campaigns: The 1950s

As the midpoint of the 20th century climaxed there were signs that the brief honeymoon which public education had enjoyed during the Second World War was over. Enrollment in elementary school was stable until the effects of the post World War II baby boom were felt in the 1950s when enrollment jumped by 36 percent. In the next decade it rose by only ten percent. As a further indication of the post World War II baby boom, high school enrollments doubled in the 1950s and did not wane until the 1980s. College enrollment figures revealed similar trends, except that they did not decrease in the 1980s. Post high school aged people were beginning to enroll in college during that period, thus boasting the average age of the college population. Based on current enrollment trends, statistics show that education is now the fastest growing business in North America.

In 1956 the research division of the National Education Association (NEA) surveyed thirty American public magazines as a means of determining public attitudes towards schooling. The top ten criticisms sketched by magazine writers were compared with and validated by research studies conducted by the NEA. At the top of the list of complaints was the notion that public school policy was in the control of professional educators. There was also concern about the deteriorating influence of progressivist ideas and the notion that life adjustment education was replacing intellectual training in the curriculum. Traditional morals and values were not being taught and subjects such as science, mathematics and language were being replaced by courses on living skills. Progressivist ideas were blamed for the practice of promoting all students supplemented by lax discipline, lack of competition and the neglect of gifted children (Stinnett and Huggett, 1963).

Despite these criticisms, many educators were optimistic that the new education would bear results which the public would not be able to ignore. Then, in 1957, the Soviet spaceship, Sputnik, became the first man-made satellite and American politicians immediately began to the clamor for stricter mental disciplining and more rigorous academic drill in schools. Critics said that schools had been lax in preparing the best intellects to take over their destined roles. Not everyone immediately agreed. In 1959 the Conant Report appeared, emanating from a study of the American comprehensive high schools in eighteen states. Conant was very positive about the format of the comprehensive high school, and recommended that smaller, rural high schools be closed down and arrangements be made for students to be bussed to the nearest urban comprehensive high school. Conant identified three essential requirements for a good school system in the United States including: (i) a school board composed of devoted, intelligent, understanding citizens who realized fully the distinction between policy making and administration; (ii) a first-rate superintendent; and, (iii) a good principal (Conant, 1959: 43).

Conant elaborated twenty-one recommendations to improve already good schools including a fully-articulated counselling system, individualized instruction, trade and vocational programs, special arrangements for gifted and academically-challenged students, an academic honors list, and the formation of homerooms. The following year Professor Myron Lieberman

(1960) criticized Conant for his strong stand against rural high schools and accused him of recommending improvements that had been recognized by others at least two decades earlier. Lieberman, of course, placed the blame for the lack of action towards improvement on teachers and school boards whom he castigated as dormant, non-reformers. He warned that if anything was going to be done about Conant's suggested reforms it would involve many meetings and long and costly experiments from which the results would have to be made available both to teachers and the public.

A few years after the Conant Report was published, Conant wrote *Education in a Divided World,* in which he admitted to a growing consciousness of the immense difficulty of ensuring that the common core curriculum which he had advocated could have the same value for all students. By now he was aware of the great diversity of American population which could be translated to mean that, in terms of insights and values, different children would have different needs. Even as the rising number of immigrant groups developed unique communities, they would also have the right to expect the schools to take cognizance of some elements of their belief systems and value preferences. With this writing, Conant gave clear indication that he was quite ready to acknowledge some of the factors that contributed to the turbulent sixties which followed.

The 1960s

Several factors contributed to the development of a more humanistic emphasis in education during this decade. The Vietnam War was questioned by those who were being called to fight in it, the phenomenon of the flower children flourished, and a new social conscience emerged featuring concern for the poor, urban decay, exploitation of natural resources, and racial inequality. Writings by such educators as John Goodlad, Paul Goodman, Ivan Illich, Ashley Montagu, A. S. Neill, Jonathan Kozol, George Leonard, Myron Lieberman, and Charles Silberman dominated the scene.

Montagu (1958) borrowed from anthropology to make the point that a more humanistic atmosphere in schools would enhance learning. George Leonard (1968) stressed that improved personal relations could be a means of producing more effective learning environments. He emphasized that learning should be a sheer delight and viewed as life's ultimate purpose. Charles Silberman (1973) insisted that the joy of learning could be attained simply by amending existing curricula and teaching methods. He promoted the notion that by building on student awareness of the trust placed in them to guide the future affairs of the nation, they would see learning as a necessary step towards fulfilling that responsibility. One common strain in the radical literature of this decade reveals that these thinkers wanted public schools to change, even though there was little agreement about the direction or nature of the proposed change. One thing was certain; under the watchful eye of these educators, schools would no longer simply be able to carry on business as usual.

As public interest in schooling increased, a variety of programs to improve education were mounted to resolve community concerns. It was assumed that schools were the property of taxpayers and they should be more responsive to local needs. An effective initiative was the establishment of parent advisory councils which were organized and occasionally called upon to offer input. Quickly the councils proved useful in matters of instruction, curriculum, community acceptance of school programs and the development of new courses of study. Frequently, their members were appointed by administrators on nomination by classroom teachers, by the district superintendent, or by the board of education. Essentially the arrangement served successfully to ward off possible community tensions about school operations and helped develop stronger community support for schools.

The push to inaugurate parent advisory groups was originally part of the American Head Start, Follow Through and Title I programs, and soon after spread to other districts as well. Often touted as the "citizen participation movement" in the United States, advocates of the concept eventually demanded to know how money was being spent in schools, whether the curriculum correlated with children's needs, and what kinds of hiring and firing practices for teachers and administrators were in place. Despite the increasing public role of these groups, some school districts mandated that parent advisory councils should be organized on a compulsory basis (Fain et al., 1979).

Always in a responsive position to accommodate public whims, schooling in the 1960s reflected the uneasiness experienced by parents who wanted their children educated in a less traditional and more humane fashion. As a result, alternative schools that could best be described as reactionary burgeoned. A number of writers denounced traditional structures and practices and posed a myriad of non-conforming experiments. Phrases like nongraded schools, open area schools and schools without walls appeared, all of which were intended to make public schools more responsive to students' needs. John Goodlad, for example, lamented that children were too much classified on the basis of grade, years of progress and the chronological stage which they occupied in the school ladder. The reality was that rarely did any two children progress at the same rate, nor did their mental age always coincide with the academic estimations made of their state or progress. Yet schools were premised on the notion that children did mature and develop at quite similar rates. Goodlad claimed that schools should get their acts together and adjust programs to this reality (Goodlad and Anderson, 1963). "

Summerhill

British educator, A. S. Neill went further than his reform-minded American colleagues in the search for child-centred alternatives, and, posed what was deemed a radical approach to child rearing even in those times. Neill argued that school itself was irrelevant and the basis of education should be that children were free to explore. He postulated that the aim of education, indeed the aim of life, should be to work joyfully and find happiness, the latter defined as being interested in life by responding freely to all of life's stimuli (Gosden, 1969).

Although Neill's residential school was built in 1921, it was not until the philosophically turbulent 1960s that much attention was given to it. The school was held in an old English country home and usually enrolled about forty-five children, aged five to sixteen. There were no formal classes, although teachers were available to act as facilitators should any student choose to consult with them. As the days progressed, Neill felt it appropriate for children to wander the halls and yard, play, or take up lessons. They could explore the terrain or "each other," for that matter, at will. Neill believed that intellectual development was only one facet of child development, and therefore the sum total of their daily experiences comprised their learning portfolios. Townhouse meetings to decide about procedures and such were frequent, and everyone, including Neill, had an equal voice in decision-making.

Although Neill was opposed to external disciplinary action of any kind, he did find it necessary to impose a few rules on his young charges. He blamed the necessity for making rules on pressures from outside by school officials who might deem his school unfit for state approval and force its closure. One such rule pertained to banning alcohol from the premises, and requiring children to wear clothing and refrain from having sex with one another. Despite these restrictions, Neill cautioned his students not to have guilt about anything they chose to do, but to experiment with and enjoy every aspect of their development. Neill felt that guilt feelings have the function of binding the child to authority, thereby starting a cycle which would oscillate constantly between rebellion, repentance, submission and new rebellion. For Neill, guilt was not the voice of conscience, but an awareness of disobedience against authority and fear of reprisal. At its best, guilt was seen to breed fear, which produced hostility and hypocrisy (Neill, 1960).

As the example of Summerhill continued to inspire copycat versions, educators publicly voiced their concerns about the experiment. In a book, *Summerhill: For and Against,* published in 1970, a series of essays by fifteen educators and social scientists decried or praised Neill's efforts. No one, it seemed, was neutral about Summerhill. Max Rafferty, a Califonria Superintendent of Public Instruction called Neill's approach educational quackery, twaddle, and phallic pagaism. He labelled Neill an "educational prostitute" because of his lackadaisical approach to heterosexual play on the school grounds (Rafferty, 1970. Neill defended his position suggesting that he was encouraging complete freedom to explore. Perhaps surprisingly, the second essay in the collection (by John M. Culkin, S.J.), supported Summerhill as a holy place, because it was void of the negative media blitz littered with assassinations, violence, war and commercials witnessed daily by American children from the time of their birth. Culkin admitted that he had only read about Summerhill and had never visited the site, but as a media consultant he was undoubtedly swayed in his support strictly by his disillusionment with the content of television programming.

Thus the arguments raged, and the support of educators like Ashley Montagu, John Holt and Erich Fromm greatly helped the cause. After Neill's death, Summerhill was managed by his daughter, Zoe Redhead, herself educated at her father's school. Most of Summerhill's imitators, however, passed from the scene, so much so that by the early 1970s one could legitimately ask the question, "Where have all the free schools gone?" (Myers, 1973).

The Summerhill of the 1990s operates in much the same way as it did during all of its seventy-five year existence. The students still run the weekly business meetings with both students and teachers having one vote each. Although the school generated some very negative press due to a biased movie made about it in 1992, it survived the portrayal as a tense, aggressive and confrontational community and continues to foster Neill's principles of love, natural development and freedom of expression (Darling, 1994).

By the 1960s a parallel reform player had entered the arena of education in America, sometimes labelled "education for self-realization." Typified by the "I gotta be me" syndrome rampant in society generally, many American youth became "flower children," questioning the nation's involvement in the Vietnam War, and expressing concern about exploitation of the earth's natural resources. Schooling was suddenly viewed as out of touch with the times and the theme of education for self-realization emerged. The campaign was premised on the following kinds of assessments; "school is a kind of jail" (Holt, 1973), "effective alternatives to schools cannot occur without other widespread changes" (Reimer, 1972), and "learning should be a sheer delight" (Leonard, 1968). Still, within a very short time, and despite the best efforts of these apostles of progress, education for self-realization completed its act and the stage was returned to business as usual. In 1979, Neil Postman (1979a) announced that the era of school reform in America was over and reluctantly admitted that the treadmill of tradition had prevailed.

The School Without Walls

As the popularity of A.S. Neill's Summerhill grew, copycat versions soon dotted the North American landscape. Every major Canadian city could boast at least one "free school," many of which lasted no more than a decade. A similar situation prevailed in the United States of which the Parkway Program was quite representative.

The founders of the Philadelphia Parkway Program were highly critical of public education, arguing that the public school alienated local community residents from high schoolers because the school was not an integral part of the community. The concern was that students were not being educated by the community, but removed from it in order to learn about it. As a result when students graduated to live in their respective communities, they were inadequately prepared to function effectively within them. Public schools might claim that they were preparing students to fulfil various professional roles after graduation, but students were not being taught how to behave as citizens in a democracy (Bremer and von Moschzisker, 1971).

The basic platform of the School Without Walls was to admit high school students to the program on the basis of their own intention, application and signature. In February, 1969, the directors prepared to admit 120 students to the new experiment, but the task to do so grew quite complex when two thousand potential students in Philadelphia requested admittance. The problem was resolved by developing an elaborate lottery system, and so the program began.

Parkway offered no formal classes as such, but students could choose from a variety of activities ranging from academics, architecture, art and computer science to learning trades such as carpentry, electrician, plumbing and sheet metal work. More feminine trades being offered included dressmaking and home economics. A tutorial arrangement was set up in community "depots" so that students could work with individuals already familiar with their field of choice even though most of them were not certified teachers. The qualification to participate as a tutor was experience and familiarity with one's field, be it law, medicine, sports or mechanics. Students set their own objectives, and a course of study was seen as complete when students decided that it was so. After the first year of experimentation, staff, students and parents expressed a high level of satisfaction with the program, and the number of applications for the second year doubled. Despite these glowing factors, some staff expressed concern that they did not always know what was going on because of the flexible schedule of the school. In addition, teachers noted that the program did not encourage meaningful interactions between black and white students after class (Cox and Lazorki, 1972).

When the director of the school, John Bremer, resigned after the second year of operation, he was given this tribute, "He has brought to Philadelphia his conviction that good education is something that happens to kids, not something packaged and passed out by teachers" (Bremer and von Moschzisker, 1971: 178). Despite this glowing testimony to Bremer's actions, the School Without Walls eventually experienced the same fate as other free schools. By the next decade, North Americans were again prepared to erect roof-covered walls in which to educate their young.

Community Schools

A quickly rising star in the crown of educational improvement in the 1960s was the community school movement, which accentuated the objective of utilizing school staff and school facilities for total community use. Willie (2000) argues that the roots of community education can be traced back to the 1920s to studies initiated by scholars in sociology at the University of Chicago who focused on demographic characteristics and ecological organization of urban communities.

The 1960s effort was greatly aided by financial support of the Mott Foundation of Flint, Michigan, so the campaign quickly spread to neighboring states and even to Canada. For a short time, community schools were very popular. Some proponents articulated the concept of the twenty-four hour school implying that many activities be added to the roster of school offerings targeted for an evening adult population. They claimed that the school had the responsibility of providing the community with additional information about their programs, securing community support for these programs, developing programs employing community resources, and meeting the expressed needs of community constituents. Proponents of the new concept envisaged community schools as a sign of hope for what was termed a dying institution (Nelson, 1973; Stamp, 1975; Galardi, 1994).

Some of the highlights of community school programs included additional involvement of parents in school programming, increased activities and responsibilities for school staff, and intense interagency cooperation with service clubs, churches and government agencies. Some schools quickly produced community newsletters and engaged in more frequent consultations with community people who acted as resource personnel in schools. Here they taught noncredit courses on such topics as health, substance abuse, crafts or sports. The underlying philosophy was that if there was community demand for a program and the necessary personnel could be put into place, virtually any kind of program could be mounted.

As long as funding for community programs was in place, the community school movement flourished. Teachers were paid for extra time spent in schools and some resource personnel were hired. The burden on the school included the provision of extra supplies, longer burning lights and maintenance costs. In some instances governments participated financially, and until the 1980s when the keyword in political circles was cutbacks, everything went well. For a short time the community school movement lent support to the notion that in a democratic nation schools belong to the community and should be available for all.

A very positive feature of community schools was that their formation greatly enhanced parental interest in the education of their children. At times parents and children attended evening school activities together and thus the parent-child bond was strengthened. Some proponents of community schools argued that through the years the very goals of education had become entangled in the rising bureaucratic shuffle that increased with the growth of public schools. By placing the control of schools back in the community where it belonged, the school could again become responsive to public needs. The desired sharing of the workload by newcomers did not always match up with the visions of those who traditionally held the reins of control, so some interesting collisions occurred. Not all school administrators were prepared for the onslaught of dozens of enthusiastic but relatively uninformed personnel who also wanted to "sit on the board," so to speak. At first the invaders were assigned to peripheral and ceremonial functions of school governance, but they gradually worked their way up even to advising on basic management of school procedures. Today only a semblance of the former momentum of a significant shift in local school management remains, a symbol of yet another attempt to improve North American education.

A contemporary example of continuing community school interest is the Community Alternative High School in Ann Arbor, Michigan, which was founded in 1972. The basic philosophy of the school remains unchanged, namely, to meet individual student needs, focus on community involvement and respect for the principle of democracy. Each student at the school is part of a smaller unit known as a forum, and this arrangement assures that every student has opportunity to speak to local and individual issues. Students are also given opportunity to have input on curriculum selection and development. Since the State of Michigan's Department of Educational fosters the principle of choice in schooling, Alternative High School personnel like to emphasize that their teachers and students are there by choice (Galardi, 1994). Thus dreams never die.

Another example of this kind of persistence spilled over into the 1990s when a group of concerned teachers and parents in Lafayette, Indiana, began a privately-sponsored New Community School (NCS). The intent was not so much to build a sense of community although it turned out that this was the most sustaining and unifying force the institution had. The initiating group believed that their form of schooling would increase parental involvement and enhance students' learning experiences. A community survey provided an initial student body of 37 students, and persistent fund-raising, low teachers' salaries and parental support kept the school going through its first year of operation (Elster et al., 1994). Although current information regarding the operation of the school is not available, the experiment demonstrates the lengths to which people will go to maintain a dream.

One of the greatest hindrances to establishing a more widespread array of community schools in the 1960s was cost, particularly in heavily-populated urban areas. Since the scope and extent of the school was increased, it meant significant readjustments to a variety of other social institutions such as welfare, policing, housing and urban renewal. Local politicians sometimes viewed community schools with suspicion, perhaps because they feared their popularity would cut in on their own locus of power. Another challenge in urban areas was to generate parental interest and organizing groups with limited financial resources. Despite these realities, there were those with who exhibited a positive outlook. Scanlon (1975), for example, observed that the increased knowledge, advances in instructional technology and improved understanding of the learning process of recent times all pointed to a better future for America's schools. Not everyone was that optimistic.

Minority Concerns

One of the most important factors affecting school performance during the 1960s emerged from the minority sector, particularly from within the African American community. Power strongholds for this group were consolidated in large eastern cities like Boston and New York. The success of this power-broking was validated by the fact that in 1967, two major cities elected African American mayors for the first time: Cleveland, Ohio, and Gary, Indiana. Although the primary targets of the search for equality centered on the business sector, it was only logical that schools be included in further attacks. A particular concern was the upgrading or eradication altogether of ghetto schools which functioned on inadequate funding and poorly qualified teachers, and fostered low attendance figures and a high dropout rate. Black leaders like Stokely Carmichael and Rap Brown advocated a program of defensiveness against the white establishment if their requests for equality were not met.

Writer Jacob Epstein warned that if the demands made by African American leaders were not heeded they might choose to intensify their actions with the end goal of controlling the major institutions of the urban centers of America. Epstein believed that the African American community had chosen the schools as their first major thrust. If successful, they would no doubt continue their campaign to capture control of other major institutions (Miller and Woock, 1970). As history has shown the campaign by African Americans to control schooling (if there ever was one), has not been fruitful and the control of the nation's major financial and social institutions is still where it has always been.

On another front, the 1960s were targeted with fears of Russian military supremacy. The fallout of Sputnik I in 1957 reached well into the 1960s and some writers, like James E. Frasier (1965), warned that competition with the Russians for control of outer space was crucial to American supremacy. Somehow the schools had something to do with that. Frasier stressed that the gravity of the situation could not be overestimated and if America failed to educate the present and immediately future generations appropriately well, they would lose their competitive edge with Soviet powers and cease to be free to educate and live as they saw fit.

On a more positive note, there were also educators who saw potential in schooling and urged teachers to make use of the privilege of educating the nation's future leaders. As Abraham (1964: 30) stated,

> Unfortunately the list of problems is much longer than any group of individuals could assemble on the basis of their own schooling. The fact that they seem overwhelming is compensated for only by the fact that we really do have the personnel, creativity and funds to do something about them.

The 1960s brought with them a healthy focus on the individuality of human beings. True, many of the psychological jingles that were originated during this time were ill-grounded in reputable theory, but writers like William Glasser (1969) patiently elevated the importance of individual learning to the place it deserved. Glasser believed that each individual student in the school system should be challenged to believe that he or she had a privilege and responsibility to work to succeed in the world and rise above any handicaps that faced them. Society, on the other hand, had the responsibility of providing a school environment in which the foregoing goal could realistically be achieved. As he put it, "Unless we provide schools where children, through a reasonable use of their capacities, can succeed, we will do little to solve the major problems of the world" (Glasser, 1969: 6). According to this viewpoint, any measure of global success to be experienced by world nations in terms of peace and goodwill, would first have to be accomplished for the individual. The belief was that healthy, enlightened, knowledgeable individuals would lend their energies towards the attainment of that same condition in situations affecting others and hence, the world.

The 1970s

When the dust had settled from the educational revolution of the previous decade, reformers became a little more helpful in making recommendations for schooling. Instead of calling for an immediate shutdown of schools or banning the institution altogether, there was a genuine posing of alternatives to traditional type learning environments. Unfortunately, by then teachers had grown weary of all the criticism channelled their way and many had burned out. Morale was low, highlighted by a series of unhealthy characteristics such as rage and helplessness, guilt, insecurity and hopelessness (Robert, 1976). Appreciation for educational theory and philosophy of education was at an all-time low and even considered irrelevant (Phillips, 2000). In a study by Ferge (1974) teachers identified the school as only fourth in order of influence in the socialization process, preceded in importance by such factors as friends (peer group), family and mass media. Zeigler and Peak (1970) concurred with the perception that schooling could best be described as a mirror of community values and not serving at all as an agent of change.

Criticisms of public schools in the 1970s essentially took three different forms. The *first* concern was a call for a return to the basics because evidence was mounting that the schools were falling down on their responsibility to teach the 3 R's. The complaint was that in the past decade too much emphasis had been placed on frills at the expense of teaching language arts and mathematics. A *second* criticism targeted rising social problems, both in society as well as in the school setting, with the charge that the schools ought to be doing something about such matters as desegregation and inequity. *Third* and finally, there were those who demanded that educators devise a comprehensive life skills program to meet the needs of the times. Viewed as a more rational approach, agitators for the life skills program perceived the need for students to be able to make sensible decisions, solve problems, clarify their value systems, understand personality development and develop meaning about the nature of the world around them. This reform movement was partially developed in response to parental demand and partly in reaction to studies that revealed declining achievements on behalf of the public school student population. The underlying assumption of this perspective was that schools needed to do more than teach the basics; they needed to prepare students how to learn and how to be prepared for lifelong learning (Ignas, 1981).

Some community groups, disconcerted by the ethical erosion evident in so many community and national sectors, demanded that schools focus on moral development. Later in the decade and at the dawn of the 1980s, other widespread serious concerns posed challenges to the system. The need for new sources of energy, the continuing world population explosion, the evolution of new communication systems and subsequent changes in lifestyle were accompanied by demands for public schools to respond to new programs with relevant changes.

Educators Philip W. Jackson, Amitai Etzioni and John Ohlinger, who had a heart for public education, admitted that the school had flaws, but these were fixable. They suggested that public literacy would be at a very low ebb except for the role of the school. They pointed to the value of the work by Paulo Freire, the Brazilian educator, who taught children to read without enrolling them in a school (Elias, 1975), but they accused the deschoolers of throwing out the baby with the bath. They saw no solid evidence to support the blanket assertion that schools had completely failed in their assignment to educate children. Schools had not failed, since most citizens could still read and they were using many of the skills they had learned in school to run their businesses (Jackson et al., 1973).

Laska (1976) expressed concern that with all of the hoopla about school success, critics were forgetting about equal opportunity for children. He cautioned that one of the most important questions to answer regarding education in America was whether or not equivalent programs for both public and secondary education should be provided across the nation. Some school districts appeared to have more financial resources available to them, and as a result students in those districts had greater advantage in attaining academic success. Since students in certain districts were ordinarily required by school system authorities to attend designated schools, it was possible for wealthier parents to choose to live in districts that had better schools. Laska pointed out that to those who believed in hereditary privilege or meritocracy, this situation appeared to be quite acceptable.

One reaction to criticisms of schooling in the 1970s gave birth to the notion of alternatives (Illich and Sullivan, 1974). Glatthorn (1975) observed that the public had finally come to believe what the doomsayers were disgruntled about and responded by starting alternative programs. The new programs emphasized a variety of themes including concerns about educational philosophy, that is, whether schools should primarily be liberal arts or vocational institutions. Investigations were launched to probe the extent to which such themes as nationalism, indoctrination, equality and religion were being emphasized in school curricula.

Cooperative Learning

An encouraging educational movement that has prevailed to this day has been labelled cooperative learning. It found its roots in the philosophy of progressivist education. Proponents pointed out that since learning goals could be structured in any of three ways – individualistically, competitively or cooperatively – it was the latter approach that best fit the needs of a democratic society. Essentially cooperative learning was a good fit for teachers who structured learning goals as a means of determining how students interacted with one another. Student interaction patterns, it was argued, exert considerable influence on instructional outcomes.

Essentially cooperative learning originated in the formation of instructional strategies designed to help students work and learn together. The approach was based on the idea that democratic nations must educate children so they can fulfil their democratic obligations and still meet their individual needs on attaining adulthood. Early studies of cooperative learning indicated that high achievement had been attained in mastery of facts, information and theories taught in school. The development of critical thinking competencies and the use of higher level reasoning strategies were also evident. Students developed positive attitudes towards learning and were motivated to pursue learning activities on their own. A great deal of emphasis was placed on the ability to utilize one's knowledge and resources in collaborative activities with other people in career, family, community and other social settings (Johnson and Johnson, 1975).

One of the advantages of cooperative learning is that the approach can be used with students of any age, in any subject area, using a variety of curriculum materials and technological aids. The approach has successfully been used with both heterogeneous and homogenous groups in situations involving gifted, medium-ability and mentally challenged students. With such flexibility, and with each learning task appropriately structured, the method allows for the ability of each student to be maximized.

Cooperative learning involves four critical aspects:

(i) Positive interdependence, which can be attained through mutual goals, division of labor, assignment of roles and by giving joint rewards;

(ii) Face-to-face interactions among students which promotes learning and social growth and maximized positive interdependence;

(iii) Individual accountability for mastering assigned materials. Feedback sessions can be useful in determining the level of mastery of each student; and,

(iv) The furtherance of appropriate interpersonal and small-group skills as a means of assuring that students will be able to participate in collaborative efforts (Johnson and Johnson, 1985).

Those who promote cooperative learning are vitally concerned with the attainment of legitimate educational objectives such as student mastery of facts, as well as the development of critical thinking competencies and the use of higher level reasoning strategies. They stress that students need to develop the ability to utilize their knowledge and resources in collaborative activities with their peers because such skills are essential for effective functioning in career, community and family settings. The attainment of success in human interaction also fosters psychological health and well-being on the part of students.

Effective Schools

As the decade of the 1970s neared its demise an energetic attempt to set things right in the public school movement emerged in the effective schools movement encouraged by such writers as John Goodlad (1983), and Ronald Edmonds and John Fredericksen (1979). The fundamental assumption propelling the effective schools movement was that schooling could be improved with the strengthening of its strong points. The concept of schooling as a unique culture was posited, suggesting that local schools should be responsible in determining their own direction. To begin the quest for this kind of autonomy the school should be careful to develop a common philosophical base upon which to make decisions and to plan for the professional development of its members.

The foundations of an effective school were to rest on the reliability of significant educational studies and feature cross-subject and cross-grade decision-making groups who would work together to determine ways to make their school more effective. A positive school ethos was promoted in school featuring consistency of practice and high achievement expectations for every student. After some research with successful effective schools, Goodlad devised a list of seven factors that would particularly enhance any school buying into the concept (Program Evaluation Section, 1984: 43):

(i) Extensive use of rewards and praise for staff and students;

(ii) Strong emphasis on learning;

(iii) Clear indications of the level of expectations that teachers had for each student;

(iv) Full student participation in all decision-making, albeit mostly in an advisory capacity;

(v) Promotion of a pleasant appearance and comfort theme in school environment;

(vi) Maximization of effective school organization and encouragement of teacher skill development; and,

(vii) Firm leadership on the part of administration and teacher involvement in decision-making.

Schools electing to develop an effective school aura naturally devised programs to fulfil their own needs. Use of rewards and praise, for example, could be translated to mean recognizing individual staff and students on their birthdays, or sending "warm fuzzies" to individuals (staff or students), on special occasions. If someone's picture appeared in a local newspaper that story might be featured on a school bulletin board. While the intent of such activities was positive, the program undoubtedly added to teachers' workloads. Many more hours were spent working with parent and student groups and there likely were times when people wondered how much longer such efforts could go on. Even teachers have physical limits.

Early results in one particular effective school revealed a dramatic increase in staff and student morale, and a marked decrease of concentration on crisis discipline to concentration on instructional improvement. Both staff and students became alerted to the importance of school success and achievement. There was a decrease in staff requests for transfers and library circulation increased. As teachers more openly shared effective classroom strategies, the student body showed an increase in scores on in-school and system-wide tests. School vandalism decreased as did staff and student absenteeism and a more positive approach towards problem-solving was evident among teachers. An overall spirit of cooperation pervaded the school (Toews and Barker, 1983).

An item of good news emanating from the effective school phenomenon was the fact that virtually any public school could improve its output by the inception of a few proven principles of effective education. The program proved that good schooling makes a difference and researchers were successful in isolating the characteristics that differentiate effective schools from those less effective. Strong leadership, exhibiting firm but not oppressive rules, combined with a structured set of lessons geared to the achievement level of students were high on the list of priorities in establishing an effective school. Above all, the expectation of success on the part of teachers, administration and student body has been hailed as the best assurance of overall success (Madaus et al., 1989).

Was Neil Postman right when he said that the school reform movement of the 1970s was over? Was the national system simply too large to make over in such a brief time? By now Postman was ready to admit that his own views had changed, and suggested that he and his critical colleagues may have been a bit harsh (Postman, 1979b). Besides, many of the would-be reformers lacked a sufficient pedagogical base from which to formulate change. Many of them were utopians, with no idea of what it was like to work in a day-to-day classroom setting. Postman noted that a display on glass-blowing could draw a larger crowd at a teachers' convention than a session on reform, so why flog a dead horse? Clearly, Postman, like many of his former fellow would-be reformers, was tired. The revolution was over.

The 1980s

As the decade of the 1980s got underway, Oldenquist (1984) identified some of the favorite targets of school critics who expected much more of the public schools than they had witnessed in the two previous decades. Student achievement, apparently, was too low. The critics blamed the shallow standards of the school along with lackadaisical attitudes on the part of parents which encouraged too much television-watching. They complained that old fashioned school curricula, concern about the Vietnam War, government interference, elimination of school prayers and decline of the family were contributing factors to low educational achievement. The clamor for new buildings, changes in government policy and increased financing did nothing to alleviate the fears of those who continued to harass the public school system.

One of the areas targeted by school critics was that of teaching approach. Apparently no one could do anything wrong in the 1960s, because both students and teachers were continually being told that everything they were doing was excellent. No criticism of any kind was welcomed in the classroom, not even constructive criticism. Critics saw the abandonment of the basics, class discipline, and homework, coupled with the "open-area" classroom as tantamount to chaos. Teachers basically went about the room trying to keep noise at a minimum and maintain peace. The curriculum consisted of playing with children, going on field-trips to McDonalds and telling puzzled parents that their children would learn to read when they were "ready to do so." Oldenquist joined his critical colleagues by insisting that the impact of relativistic philosophy inspired the educational objective that feeling good about oneself was the main goal of education. Any gesture to improve minority communities by imposing a work ethic or standard English on their students could be seen as a diabolical plot on the part of white, middle-class Americans who did not sufficiently respect cultural diversity. Tyack and Hansot (1984) note that the tempestuous `60s and `70s also caused the curriculum to blossom to include a myriad of elective subjects, but without any heed to an overall plan of coherence. Eclecticism was the order of the day.

As the theme of cutbacks overwhelmed the 1980s, many North Americans simply gave up on school reform and generally lost faith in public institutions. As one observer described the public mind in the 1980s: "Being a citizen today is essentially a spectator sport. Citizenship education is little more than learning what others do to make and execute the policies of government" (Lucas, 1984: 395). As an indication of this stance, voter registrations decreased and opinion polls reflected a failing confidence in government. This reality set would-be reformers to adopt a new tack; instead of railing on about failing academic standards, they stressed the need to redefine the aims of schooling in terms of citizen education in a dawning era of global interdependence. Implicit throughout was the assumption that global cooperation would follow from awareness and understanding. The new focus took attention away from the usual theme that "the schools are in a state of crisis" and instead drew attention to the implications of the shrinking reality of the international globe.

Quest for Change

The pendulum of educational reform did not stop entirely during the 1980s, but the innovations requiring additional funding of any sort certainly drew to a halt. This decade was highlighted by cutbacks, downsizing and, in too many cases, limited vision. Even the four basic essentials of public schooling became fuzzy. The *first* of these was almost completely ignored, namely that pertaining to the need to continually formulate and clarify the system of thought or basic underlying assumptions (philosophy of education) that serves as a tiller for educational process and change. *Second,* a fundamental component that was ignored or overlooked was the recognition of the tendency to mold schooling according to some perceived social need, depending on the strength of influence of a particular lobbyist group. Schools deserve better than that. *Third,* the need to foster the continuing fundamentals of learning, that is, curriculum and methodology and the fulfillment of students' needs and expectations was downplayed. *Fourth* and finally, there was the matter of what could be perceived as a more extraneous feature like school management and the professional status of teachers; this too received little print. Typical of the 1980s trend to look inward for reform targets, one writer, A. E. Soles (1988) emphasized the central concerns of schooling to be the status of the teaching profession, student evaluation, teacher-student ratio, and teacher participation in school governance. Regardless of social mood or the nature of proposed reforms, the components identified by Soles remain as vital to the very existence and basic functions of the nation's educational institutions.

As hard times struck the continent, the public mind turned to the task of finding a way to generate additional monies for school sustenance and needed projects. Schools were criticized for not concentrating on job training because so many graduates were without employment during this decade. In a public survey conducted in Ontario in 1985 respondents representing the body politick were asked to rank what they perceived to be the top priorities of public schools. Numeracy and computer skills were ranked as basics needed by all students because they were perceived to be the most productive skills in obtaining employment. A majority of respondents indicated that business and vocational studies should be made compulsory for students intending to enter either community colleges or the work force. While high schools were being charged with obligations to train youth for the job market, higher values were also placed on post-secondary training. A survey conducted in the United States in 1978 indicated that only 36 percent of people polled indicated that a college education was very important to economic success. By 1985 this figure had risen to 64 percent (Livingstone and Hart, 1987).

As the final death knell for the 1980s sounded, many observers wondered why the posed reforms seemed so ineffectual. Analysts discovered that public schools were proceeding on very much as they did before the proposed revolution of the two previous decades. There were still classes to attend, lessons to be learned and examinations to be passed. With a few possible exceptions, schools now offered designated smoking areas for students with the remainder of the facilities looking much the same as they had for half a century. What, if anything had changed?

No one had to wait long for the proverbial other shoe to drop. Already there were reformers at work, this time operating within the parameters of the public school system itself with the goal of creating legitimate alternatives in the form of charter schools. The reformers were joined by state officials who began slowly to wrest power from the American federal government by creating local policies and redesigning new curriculum and instructional procedures which had previously been the province of local school boards and educators. Some observers criticized state officials for acting as superschool boards, telling school districts and superintendents how to manage schools. Although even today the federal government in Canada has no direct responsibility for what goes on in the schools, its impact in the 1980s was strongly felt through its funding to the provinces and through the implementation of social programs. Innovations such as the federal policy on bilingualism and biculturalism and the entrenchment of the Charter of Rights obligated provincial governments to develop educational policies in accord with federal legislation (Ghosh and Ray, 1987).

State funding for education did not increase substantially during the 1980s, but state officials were on the lookout to see how the lavish grants of the 1970s would be utilized. Accountability was the order of the day. Murphy (1990) speculated that the public also began to look to the state for direction, having grown weary of special interest groups who had too much say in educational matters. In Canada, for example, the trend toward centralization tended to concentrate decision-making power in the upper and restricted spheres of government bureaucracies (Livingstone and Hart, 1987). In the United States, the move signified the re-emergence of faith in the connection between education and the economic well-being of the states at a time when many of them found themselves in financial jeopardy, but were still expected by the federal government to solve their own problems.

The essential ingredient of the school reform movement of this decade was a healthy emphasis on improving public schooling, not dismantling it. For the first time in history scholars trained in organizational theory and educational policy were called on to make suggestions for improvement. They studied standard-raising, investigated opportunities to learn and made recommendations about redirection of attention, resources and energy towards maximizing the known conditions of learning. One distinct difference that resulted was that schools became narrower and more academically linked. Teachers were more concerned with undertaking fewer activities, but doing them well. A focus on student outcomes, both of quality and equity, became the defining characteristic of effective schooling.

Another emerging emphasis in the 1980s was the "schools for excellence movement" (Warren, 1990), which was a reaction to an emphasis on equality of educational opportunity triggered in the 1960s. The academic achievement of students was shown to have dropped over the previous two decades, and international comparisons placed North American students well below students in other countries. In response, attempts were made to require more rigor in mathematics and science. Additional homework was assigned and the school day was extended. The range of electives was cut back and a core curriculum was established.

By the 1984-85 school years, not two years after the report, *A Nation at Risk* appeared, forty-one American states had increased requirements for high school graduation and twenty-two states had implemented some sort of competency testing. A few states also began programs designed to test individuals who wanted to enter the ranks of the teaching profession. Alternatives to public education were still being explored with rising enrollments in home schooling an indicator of continued dissatisfaction with public schooling.

The 1990s

Like the preceding decades, the 1990s were earmarked by criticisms of public schooling and, once again, the schools were seen to be in crisis (Wotherspoon, 1998). Charges levied by disconcerted critics included this list: schools were too costly to maintain in their present form, too much attention was placed on frivolous programs to the neglect of the basics, there was not enough discipline nor respect for traditional values in schools, and school personnel needed to be more responsive to the public. No doubt still reeling from financial cutbacks in the 1980s, these complaints reflected the frustration of those who sought change in an economic sense, quite impervious to educational improvements. Attempts to silence would-be reformers included the charge that those who spoke out on behalf of education were usually teachers and administrators who had vested interests in the institution.

Financial support for public schools was still somewhat strained during the 1990s, motivating a return to an emphasis on accountability for monies invested in education. Fundamental to ensuing debates about the goals and purposes of education was concern about which sectors of society education should serve. Complaints about poor returns on educational investments were substantiated by national test scores showing how poorly students had done on the tests. North of the 49th parallel the Economic Council of Canada encouraged participation in programs utilizing standardized tests in such areas as mathematics, reading and writing. A parallel move towards a national curriculum and core curricula mounted in several provinces as a means of providing specified areas of study and learning materials for all learners at particular stages in their educational journeys (Wotherspoon, 1998).

The mild educational revolution of the 1990s focussed on the development of alternatives within the system; hence the continued proliferation of charter schools. Advocates of this approach argued that public schools needed to be loosened up and become more flexible and more responsive to student needs. By concentrating on more specific approaches to learning via the establishment charter schools it was felt that the best of both private and public schooling could be offered to the constituency. It was considered the best option for those disillusioned with public schooling since it was tax-based and therefore quite affordable. Private schools could cost a lot of money, and home schooling was not always feasible for working parents. By 1995, twenty states had enacted charter school legislation, beginning with the state of Minnesota. In 1994 Alberta became the first province in Canada to authorize charter schools. Two years later eight charter schools were in operation in Alberta. The in-house revolution was under way.

Three

The Philosophical Whimsy of Public Education

Throughout the rather brief history of public schooling, pressures to influence its philosophical orientation have originated from many different sectors. Reformers have often tried to redirect the course of school instruction, usually by recommending a change in objectives, content or teaching style. At times the initial call for change has been singular, like that of a lone voice crying in the wilderness, but frequently the forces have rallied to incorporate national concerns which have effected significant alterations to public school philosophy and operations. As the servant of the people, however, schooling has always been responsive to public demands, and much more reflective of public whimsy than careful philosophical or pedagogical deliberation. Sadly, this orientation has fairly consistently resulted in a complete disregard of educational ends. As John Dewey's so adroitly warned:

> The difference between educational practices that are influenced by a well-thought out philosophy, and practices that are not so influenced is that between education conducted with some clear idea of the ends in the way of ruling attitudes of desire and purpose that are to be created, and an education that is conducted blindly, under the control of customs and traditions that have not been examined or in response to immediate social pressures. This difference does not come about because any effort to clarify the ends to be attained is, as far as it goes, philosophical. (John Dewey in Archambault, 1964: 17)

Donna Kerr (1976) once described an incident in which a school board suddenly decided to promote the establishment of a district office for the evaluation of teachers. There was no premeditation regarding possible reasons for the action, and, naturally, teachers were shocked when they heard of the proposal. It was a haphazard plan which implied that a number of teachers were behaving unprofessionally. Students quickly endorsed the concept, convinced that it would weed out teachers whose style they did not like. Community members went along with the plan, undoubtedly convinced that such action would improve education. When the school board got wind of the support for their idea, they immediately set about implementing it. The problem was they did not have any specific idea about how to proceed. John Dewey would undoubtedly have used this story to illustrate the intent of his warning about operating according to public whim rather than being motivated by a well thought-out philosophy of education.

Although Dewey is often saluted as the most influential American philosopher of the twentieth century, his warning that educational programs be based on a series of consistent, logical philosophical presuppositions went largely unheeded in the latter half of the twentieth century. Instead, one can easily trace the puppet-like reactions of public education to public moods highlighted by a series of ideological pendulum swings. True, it may be argued that the schools belong to the people, and this is as it should be in a democracy, but common sense also dictates that no public institution in North America could develop any degree of longevity if the formation of its policies were left entirely to the "person-on-the-street." If that were the case, why establish teachers' colleges or university faculties of education? Why not simply take frequent public polls by which to determine philosophy and policy?

Concern about school operations is not surprising since schools are largely responsible for the socialization of the young who are often depicted as a nation's most prized resource. Schools are also targeted for social reform because they are viewed as an easy market for a variety of business products ranging anywhere from notepaper to computers. In the context of reform per se, many people think that schools should be responsible for handling problematic phenomena. Many schools do try to meet that challenge and attempt to prepare the young for future adult challenges by incorporating a myriad of "newer" subjects such as anger management, conflict resolution, democratic decision-making or control of harmful substances into the curriculum.

Identifying Basic Perspectives

Three basic philosophical perspectives appear to have influenced the operation of public schools during the twentieth century and furnished the framework for related educational reforms. These are traditionalism, vocationalism and progressivism, and the proponents of all three perspectives have focussed on the rudiments of the learning process relevant to public thinking of the time.

The juxtaposing of the three streams of thought continued in North America until the restlessness of the 1960s brought every school activity under question. The resulting see-saw effect has had schools hopping in every direction, but always in response to public pressure and the economic sector. Traditionalists have consistently defended the aims which were drafted when schooling first originated. These included instruction in the 3 R's, at first when the primary content was classic literature, which contained the thoughts of great minds. The procedures by which these conceptualizations were to be appropriated almost always included memorization and rote. Mental discipline was a much touted notion with added emphasis on logical deduction and difficulty. Some proponents perceived that if the learning process could be rendered more complex it would somehow become meaningful and worthwhile. Participants in this pedagogical ordeal can certainly testify to its lingering cognitive value, even though the memory may be more negative than positive.

Mental discipline and faculty psychology both have their roots in the European tradition propounded by such thinkers as seventeenth century English philosopher, John Locke. Locke advocated that the English "gentleman" could be produced via rigorous processes that included the careful selection of sense data to impact on the child's "blank tablet mind." Sensations would produce ideas and then habits which would guarantee the formation of proper character. Early North American educators emulated Locke's ideas but two questioning bodies of thought surfaced at the end of the nineteenth century. One such stream was vocationalism and the other was progressivism, both of which will be dealt with later in more detail. Vocationalism emerged in response to the perceived need to prepare students for the world of business. Advocates of this persuasion feared that too much wrestling with the classics would produce a fixation for abstractions rather than furnishing marketable or employable skills.

As vocationalism spurred itself away from classical rote, simultaneously the ideas of progressivism claimed the scene. Their emphasis was on the "whole child," implying that the everyday life experiences of the child should constitute the curriculum. Critics accused the progressivists of going soft on education offering no structure other than encouraging children to indulge in fantasies. In their counter claims the progressivists insisted that children were simply being encouraged to express themselves with teachers acting as facilitators, not viewers. Progressivist John Dewey, however, insisted that if children were left alone to express themselves without guidance, any growth they experienced would simply be accidental. According to Dewey, progressivism did rely on a form of structure, but his critics were too busy to consider it.

Traditionalsim

Traditionalism was reaffirmed during the midpoint of the twentieth century with the writings of Arthur Bestor, James Koerner, Max Rafferty and Hilda Neatby. In 1953, in a book entitled Educational Wastelands, Bestor (1953) decried the inroads of modern thinking on school activity and defended what critics called the old regime. His thoughts were quite representative of that sector of public thinking who wanted to preserve the intellectual elements of education. Opponents of this view saw the move towards technicalization in America as a reason for schools to shift to a more modern emphasis on skills instead of rhetoric. Bestor promoted the notion that students could best be taught how to think by absorbing the contents of the classics. He accused progressivists of watering down the essence of education by rejecting content. Bestor argued that without meaningful content there would be no data by which to practice reasoning. Furthermore, it would be impossible for students to learn to think without having something to think about. Valued content, rather than personal experiences would have to be mastered, purely and simply.

Another representative of traditionalism, California State Superintendent Max Rafferty (1963), promoted the values of religion and patriotism along with the 3 R's. He waged a war for content in curriculum and ridiculed the notions of life adjustment and what he termed educational frills. Rafferty reacted to the inclusion of civics and economics in school curriculum insisting that history and geography should not be contaminated with what were only current relevancies. A number of schools reacted with renewed vigor to Rafferty's claims and began to emphasize elements of a traditional curriculum. They suddenly did not want to appear interested in the immediate or felt needs of students. A stress on subject matter became the watchword in traditionally-oriented schools and memorization was endorsed as a legitimate means of appropriating it.

James D. Koerner (1963) took the campaign for the maintenance of traditionalism to the arena of teacher education. He argued that high standards of learning could only be assured in public schools if more attention was given to the training of teachers. He accused educators of operating in a philosophic vacuum with no idea as to what the purpose of schooling was nor where it was headed. He targeted John Dewey and insisted that Dewey had violated his own warning by making only a few discernable bridges between his philosophical ideas and the practices which he advocated. For Koerner, the incorporating of progressivist ideas would only weaken the few bridges that could be drawn between valued philosophical assumptions and educational practice. There was no option but to reinstate academic rigor in the classrooms beginning with teacher education. Despite these charges, Dewey continued to warn educators against the practice of adopting new teaching methods on a whim, and consistently pled for teachers to examine the underlying premises of any advertised new approach.

Canadians were subject to much of the same philosophy albeit the names of the players were a bit different. A college professor, Frank MacKinnon (1962) peddled the popular myth that "anyone could get into a faculty of education," a criticism intended to imply that the level of academic standards for teacher education was exceedingly low. MacKinnon claimed that would-be teachers deliberately avoided studying business because it was too hard. A thorough-going traditionalist, he decried the lack of standards in public schools as well as the poor quality of delivery by ill-prepared teachers. His approach was to enhance teacher training with rigorous mental exercise. A history professor at the University of Saskatchewan, Neatby (1953) was not so generous. She contended that very little good could come out of the teaching profession since its representatives had done such a poor job of delivering quality education. A favorite Neatby target was the so-called "education expert" whom she described as a symbol of the times in the sense of that position merely reflecting a general lowering of standards and "going soft" in Canadian society. Neatby despised the development of what she termed "educational jargon" which did nothing to help students handle the challenge of a traditional curriculum. The humanization of the curriculum, advocated by such writers as Theodore Brameld, signalled the downfall of any meaningful content in the curriculum. Again, a number of school districts responded by strengthening their grip on traditional notions of academic rigor.

The Great Books Approach

Critics and dissenters aside, the traditional education movement also attracted a group of serious-minded reformers who argued that the way to return to the basics as a means of salvaging society, was via a study of the great ideas of the past. Robert Hutchins (1953) of the University of Chicago became a particularly strong advocate of the "Great Books Approach" with Jacques Maritain and Mortimer Adler adding a special concern for the spiritual component of this intellectual pursuit.

Adler's work provides a good starting point for this discussion, particularly his contribution to the Forty-First Yearbook of the National Society for the Study of Education wherein he described the ultimate ends of all education as being "the same for all men at all times and everywhere" (Adler, 1942: 197). Adler railed against the progressivists, who by now had grabbed the attention of educators in the United States, and accused them of promoting children's experiences as justifiable curriculum content. Adler insisted that only a study of worthy ideas could liberate the human mind, not childish experiences. The Great Books, according to Adler, contained ideas that are universal, transcultural and capable of motivating discussions to the highest order of reason. By studying the masters of intellect it would be possible to identify absolute universal moral principles by which to guide societal functions. Adler employed the term "absolute" in the sense that philosophy is not relative to the contingent circumstances of time and place, and he used the term "universal" in the sense that these ideas are not concerned with essentials and abstracts from any and every sort of merely accidental variation (Adler, 1942). Thus the derivation of a philosophy of education by which to guide the operation of public schools would be entirely dependent upon first principles from which educational objectives and methodologies would spring.

In his book, *How to Read a Book* (1940) Adler reflected the traditionalists' complaint that the schools of the times failed to promote high academic standards. By yielding to progressivist pressures, testing of students showed that high school graduates were unable to pass minimal tests of literacy. Although Adler had studied with John Dewey, he found the lure of Robert Hutchins' thinking much more satisfying. He joined Hutchins in amassing a list of the Great Books of all time. He was also instrumental in developing the Syntopicon as an index to the main ideas of the Great Books. Ironically, John Dewey was the only American whose works were included on Adler's list.

Although proponents of the Great Books loved to criticize the progressivists for using mushy and meaningless language, consider the poetic imagery of this passage:

> What is liberal education?. . . It is not an education that teaches a man how to do any specific thing. . . . this is what liberal education is. It is the education that prepares us to be free men. You have to have this education if you are to be happy, for happiness consists in making the most of yourself. You have to have this education if you are going to be a member of the community; for membership in the community implies the ability to communicate with others. You have to have this education if you are going to be an effective citizen of a democracy; for citizenship requires that you understand the world in which you live and that you do not leave your duties to be performed by others, living vicariously and vacuously on their virtue and intelligence. A free society is a society composed of free men. To be free you have to be educated for freedom. (Adler and Wolff, 1959: v-vi)

The Great Books people demonstrated great faith in the power of reason derived from knowledge as a basis for social reform. Hutchins insisted that if schools were to be charged with setting moral objectives for society, any application of those ideas would merely reflect the ideas of those who promoted them. Thus it behoved society to implement principles based on the best ideas of all time. Naturally these ideas were contained in the Great Books. Hutchins agreed with Plato that governments reflect human nature which is predicated on universal knowledge and not subject to time and space (or place) and if pursued, must constitute the basis of humankind becoming what we are capable of becoming, namely free (Hutchins, 1953).

Most educators of the time ridiculed what they perceived to be the narrow focus of the Great Books approach, whose proponents retaliated with vigor to all criticisms. Robert Hutchins himself was accused of being a moral idealist and an absolutist in a time when relativity was on a high roll. In Hutchins' defense, it must be acknowledged that he, like John Dewey, believed that educational aims should be derived from studied metaphysical beliefs, lest education be conducted with no idea of why certain content or procedures should be endorsed. The two differed in that Hutchins perceived the need of education to be wisdom and goodness while Dewey insisted that the major goal of education was the continuous reconstruction of experience. Unfortunately, the two thinkers were not particularly on speaking terms so that their differences could be discussed and perhaps resolved.

One of the primary concerns in American education has been the preparation of the young to be able to function effectively in a democracy. Traditionalists and progressivists alike claimed to have found a workable approach to the challenge but their approaches were in stark contrast to each other. Dewey's passion for equal opportunity led him to support the notion of heterogeneous grouping in schools based on the premise that the less able would be able to benefit from the knowledge of their more knowledgable peers. Adler, on the other hand, readily admitted that since individuals are not equally endowed with intelligence, not all people would be capable of benefitting from discussions of great ideas. He anticipated criticism on this point and hastened to add that all humankind was probably capable of being educated to the point of being able to be good citizens. Adler hoped that this position would accommodate the principle of "government by the people" but did not impede the development of those with leadership potentialities beyond those of the average "educable citizen" (Adler, 1964). Dewey must have cringed at that statement.

Updating Traditionalism

As the philosophical war waged on between traditionalists and progressivists, Jerome S. Bruner (1963) undertook a synthesis of the two perspectives in a book called, *The Process of Education*. Bruner attempted to make the point that children could justifiably be confronted with the rudiments of a basic liberal education early in their development. He contended that any subject could effectively be taught in some intellectually honest form to young children. He agreed with the progressivists that children should be assisted in the process of discovery learning, but maintained that a good curriculum also stresses definite structure, but not details. Structure was meant to imply that all content is related which is different than the notion that curriculum is a series of discrete pieces of knowledge. Individuality in education would be accommodated by encouraging students to discern relationships between elements of knowledge personally. Once the structural concept was comprehended, students would be able to transfer their understanding to other areas of interest. As a result students would be motivated to seek structure (relationships) within the fields of their experience. Equipped with structural insight, students would be able efficiently and effectively to utilize whatever specific information was at hand (Ornstein and Hedley, 1973).

Traces of progressivism could be identified in Bruner's works, particularly when he suggested principles like the following:

> ... intellectual growth involves an increasing capacity to say to oneself and others, by means of words or symbols, what one has done or what one will do, [and] growth depends upon internalizing events into a 'storage system' that corresponds to the environment. (Bruner, 1966: 5)

Clearly, the earmarks of respect for individualized insight were evident in Bruner's philosophy, but his underlying conceptualization of a "basic" structure of incorporated knowledge (which is metaphysically "outside of the students") should have gone a long way toward appeasing the traditionalists' conceptualization of absolute knowledge.

The Spiritual Dimension

Although traditionalists made a great deal of the notion of absolute truth and knowledge, only a few writers made allowances for the emanation of truth from Theistic sources. Hence it was up to the NeoThomists, revivalist followers of Thomas Aquinas, to add that component to the discussion. Best known among such writers is the work of Jacques Maritain (1943) who delivered the memorable Terry Lectures at Yale University in the early 1940s and published in book form under the title, *Education at the Crossroads*. Essentially anti-progressivist in conviction, Maritain lambasted educators for neglecting the ends of the occupation and promulgating a grievous misconception of the nature of humankind. In true NeoThomist style, Maritain posited a twofold nature of humankind based on reason and revelation.

> Thus the fact remains that the concepts of and integral idea of man which is the prerequisite of education can only be a philosophical and religious idea of man. I say philosophical, because this idea pertains to the nature or essence of man; I say religious, because of the existential status of this human nature in relation to God and the special gifts and trials and vocation involved. (Maritain, 1943: 6)

Maritain readily conceded the existence of many different religious concepts of humankind but clarified that his own perspective was molded from Greek, Jewish and Christian influences. This view postulates that people are animals endowed with reason whose supreme dignity is in the intellect; yet humankind is free in personal relation with God whose supreme righteousness consists in voluntarily obeying the laws of God. Maritain lamented that Robert Hutchins did not go far enough in his metaphysical enunciations because he did not take into account the facts about people and their destiny which has been made known to humankind through revelation. According to another NeoThomist, Thomas McGuckin, without this acknowledgement, metaphysics has no base, no roots. McGuckin charged Hutchins in this manner:

> To quote Thomas Aquinas as Hutchins does, without taking cognizance of the additions he made to Aristotle's thought is to quote an Aquinas who never existed. Without reference to Aquinas' thoughts on Revelation, there is no Aquinas. (McGuckin, 1942: 251)

The educational implications of the NeoThomist stance were that a wholistic concept of humankind can be derived only by calling into play the totality of people's powers – moral, intellectual and physical – by and for their individual and social uses, directed towards the union of these activities with their Creator as their final end. For the NeoThomists, traditional education implied doing the job right – assuring a liberal curriculum and an appeal to all of the student's powers.

The notion of injecting elements of the spiritual dimension into school ongoings has not been quieted. Although a more global perspective is being touted today, promoters of what is known as inclusive schooling are arguing that an holistic approach to teaching necessarily involves all components of human life – physical, emotional, intellectual and spiritual. These educators suggest that teaching practices are more productive when they are conducted in a holistic manner. Claims are made that spirituality promotes initiative and self-reflective thought. The development of a spiritual conscience can help students understand the relationship between self and the community. The underlying premise of this new approach may not sit well with traditional religionists, however, because promoters of inclusive schooling are saying that spiritual knowledge is socially constructed and changes as new knowledge and understandings are generated (Sefa Dei et al., 2000: 82-86).

Progressive Education

The first significant campaign against the mundane operations of the classic one-room schoolhouse came from the progressivists. Not content with the preoccupation of the school with teaching the rudiments of literacy and assuring the inculcation of prevailing norms, the progressivists were concerned with the individual child. They wanted children's needs to be met, their interests accounted for, and their feelings and attitudes considered in determining curriculum activities. This meant that the role of the teacher would be redrafted to that of guide or facilitator, rather than an imparter of truth, and students would become active participants in a problem-solving process rather than merely absorbers of content. The reformers were also concerned about classroom atmosphere, arguing that harsh punishment and rigidity were not as conducive to learning as an understanding and support-ive orientation on the part of the teacher. Learning procedures would also have to be modified to allow for and to encourage student input based par-tially on life experiences and partly on "research" conducted by students.

The underlying assumptions for these proposals startled the educational world to a new reality. John Dewey actually believed that children had some-thing to offer the educational process, and he was prepared to take steps to incorporate their insights. In searching for appropriate furniture for his labo-ratory school at the University of Chicago in 1897, Dewey was informed that the only kind of desks available were rows of desks bolted together. Apparently, this form of furniture was what good education was all about (Archambault, 1964: 50). The grounds on which Dewey made his defense of student input was premised on entirely different concepts of human nature and learning than had previously been acknowledged. He conceptualized learning as an interactive process in which learners interacted with their envi-ronments, social or material, and were influenced by it in a reciprocal fash-ion. Learning was not to be perceived as a passive process for children who would be called on to participate in it. Children were not to be equated with milk bottles waiting to be filled with the products of learning. Dewey con-ceived of truth and value in the same sense, allowing for the interpretations of people to influence what "really is," if it can be known, claiming that indi-viduals act not according to what is known, but according to the way they perceive each confronting situation (Bayles and Hood, 1966). Dewey defined human nature in terms of a basic neutrality, suggesting that traditional notions of depravity and moral deprivation were basically reflective of cul-tural interpretations.

A fundamental commitment to democracy was also central in progres-sivist thinking. The concomitant objective was to promote an environment wherein even "the least" would feel welcome; the plan would be to build a society where

> . . . men with minor gifts of the intellect can feel equality in all their claims for development and a decent life, can escape exploitation, use their faculties with a feeling of self-respect, gain the reward they deserve, and live as citizens . . . (Ulich, 1966: 64-65)

An irritant to the progressivists was the exclusivity of nineteenth century education which featured the selection of students solely on the basis of aca-demic achievement. The progressivist interpretation of democratic education was that a maximum of common experience and a minimum of segregation was desirable, and both academic and vocational education should be post-poned until students were at the age where selection would be better justified (Phillips, 1955). Some progressivists were entirely against the segregation of students on any count.

The child-centred approach promulgated by the progressivists found ample support in the advancement of the social sciences including child study and adolescent psychology. Correctly interpreted, it was not a campaign for children's rights, but rather belief in the ability of individuals of a young age to become self-governing (Cremin, 1961); their belief point was that the process of self-determination should be introduced gradually, not merely on attaining adulthood. Central to the concept was a healthy respect for childhood: *first,* respecting and accepting children as human beings; *second*, because they would already have accomplished feats of growing, the like of which even their teachers might never have achieved; and, *third*, because they had the potential to make a contribution to humankind (Wees, 1971). The process by which to assure this development was through inquiry – differentiating, analyzing, ordering, and synthesizing experience rather than merely listening, writing, and regurgitating (Wees, 1967).

In progressivist influenced schools, curriculum content switched quickly to a study of problems, issues and social trends as a means of acquainting the children with their immediate world. The grounds on which these phenomena evolved, namely values, were also given consideration even to the extent of questioning the nature of values, selection of fundamental values, the classification of values, value standards, and whether values were merely subjective desires or whether there was some law or norm applicable to desire. Opposition to this approach rose quickly, critics claiming that students should be taught content rather than process, and, further, they could hardly be meaningfully engaged in solving social problems when so young. The traditional purpose of schooling was to prepare students for the world they would eventually participate in as adults; it was not a place to play grown up games.

If the critics were harsh with the progressivists, their campaign was at least partially motivated by the radical departures they made with the established intellectual routines. On the more extreme edge of the movement were the reconstructionists who frightened the public even more with their announcements to build a new social order via schooling. This was certainly no way to exploit the traditional bastion of socialization and the critics minced neither words nor time in promoting that opinion.

Building a New Social Order

Few articles in the Progressivist Education Association's journal, *The Social Frontier,* were as controversial as those authored by George S. Counts, Harold Rugg, William H. Kilpatrick, and John L. Childs, largely because they conceptualized the public school as responsible for the development of a society that would be more responsive to individual needs. Although *The*

Social Frontier never printed a statement that clearly delineated the specific goals of the social reconstructionists, Counts and his colleagues made it clear what their visions for the future were. Essentially, the group was directly concerned with the moral effect of capitalism on the individual; they believed that the profit motive had a particularly pernicious effect on individual morality. Kilpatrick was especially critical of the trend and wanted to create a new system of social values that would alter the manner in which society distributes its wealth (Bowers, 1969). Counts agreed that schooling cannot rest with giving children an opportunity merely to study contemporary society but it must also lead them to becoming active in molding the future. This could best be accomplished through encouraging their contemplative and visionary capabilities. Truly the metaphysician, Counts was not very precise in explicating his own ideals for the new social order, stressing only that students should be given opportunity to participate in the fullest and most thorough understandings of the world. No suppression or distortion of facts supporting any theory or point of view should occur in their analysis of social problems. Counts castigated the view that humankind is the victim of rapid social change and helpless to do anything about it. He conceded that the forces of massive technicalizations have a way of appearing to outwit people by the very machines they have created, and ached for the development of an enlightened citizenry to take charge of both their present and their future. Such an orientation could only be assured via the inauguration of the problem-solving process in early education as well as maintaining a dedication to the concept of life-long learning (Counts, 1963).

About a decade after the social reconstructionists emerged, educator-philosopher Theodore Brameld (1965) reaffirmed their message by emphasizing a new urgency and an enlarged agenda to include such topics as international conflict, overpopulation, use of natural resources, and other encompassing themes. He envisaged the eventual development of a world civilization and projected the quick formation of world government and a universal educational system to pave the way for what he saw as both logical and inevitable. The fundamental premises of this undertaking would include respect for human dignity, and respect for all races, castes, and classes. Brameld was prepared to explicate both objectives and curriculum for this monumental undertaking, never flinching in the face of criticism that he was proposing an unrealistic and possibly naive attitude toward the potential of education in resolving world issues.

The Canadian Connection

Although the progressive education movement made much less extensive inroads on the Canadian educational scene, there were voices that paid tribute to many of the basic assumptions of the theory. In Alberta, educational philosopher Hubert Newland spoke to many audiences extolling the virtues of such concepts as education as growth, child development as total rather than segmental, and goal-centred education, offering Canadians much the same philosophical fare as Dewey and his associates in the United States. An Alberta classroom teacher, Donalda Dickie, designed a project-centred curriculum approach known as the enterprise method which reflected progressivist ideas but fell short of developing direct links to the underlying philosophy of education. In Nova Scotia, school superintendent Loren DeWolfe placed great stress on what he called "experience-centred" education, even though his constituents were more concerned about the application of learning to making a living in that region of the country. DeWolfe incorporated a real concern for teacher education and welfare in his portfolio of reform, even though his efforts fell short of any analysis of either the profession's status or authority. In so far as the implementation of progressivist ideas in Canada was concerned, the situation could best be described as a fragrance that permeated the nostrils of the enterprise of schooling without seriously affecting its direction or makeup. There is ample evidence, however, that today's educational atmosphere in Canada is more receptive to progressivist ideas than it was when the movement was in vogue.

Vocational Education

A third stream of 20th century educational thought and practice emerged in North America during the time of industrialization. Leaders in business and industry looked to the schools as important suppliers for a specialized labor force, believing that education founded on the classics was hopelessly obsolete in a modern industrial age. They were also concerned about the mass of students who would not go beyond minimal literacy training and never become scholars. Was there a place in the nation for their energies and, if so, in what ways could they best be prepared for the non-scholarly role?

In Canada, the vocational movement began with the efforts of James L. Hughes and John Seath. The latter's interest in "manual training," as the theme was known, came about in 1889 when he visited systems of secondary education in some of the principal cities of the eastern United States. These schools were quite separate from academic schools, an arrangement which appealed to Seath and which he advocated in three subsequent reports to the Ontario Department of Education. Like Hughes, Seath was affected by the Industrial Revolution which he saw as providing an opportunity to a country that was prepared to educate its youth in a way that would maximize their potentialities. By 1911 Ontario had a new Conservative Government which quickly passed Whitney's Industrial Education Act and prepared the way for Ontario's economy to make the shift from an agricultural economy to an industrial base. Hughes, who was also involved with the advancement of manual training, promoted it on the grounds that it allowed for the total education of the student. Like the NeoThomists who argued for spiritual input, Hughes claimed that manual training took cognizance of a forgotten element in the child's development. Always the Froebelian (Whilhelm Froebel was the strongest promoter of the kindergarten system in Germany), Hughes saw manual training as a natural follow-up to the play activities of the kindergarten and as the starting point for other kinds of development.

One or Two Systems

Proponents of the classicists sought to disallow the implementation of vocational schools in American education because they regarded such programs as noneducational in every sense. The progressivists were of various minds on the subject, although John Dewey did take a clear stand on the question early in his career. The central debate raged about the question as to whether or not schools designed to prepare students for the job market should be incorporated into traditional systems. One critic of the two-systems concept, Frank Tracy Carleton, voiced opposition to the "factory stage" kind of education whereby children would be processed by educational machinery to fit predetermined slots in a mass-produced system. David Snedden, on the other hand, felt it to be a happy coincidence that human beings could be sorted by ability levels parallelling the hierarchical work requirements of modern society. This way citizenry could be fitted into the place they would eventually occupy in society by virtue of their abilities by previous groundwork provided via schooling. Snedden suggested that the first few elementary grades should be the deciding levels at which such differentiation should begin. Dewey countered this claim pointing out that the question of industrial education is fraught with consequences for the future of equality and democracy. He argued that if a unified system were maintained, democracy would be honored, but a two-systems approach would accentuate undemocratic forces already at work in the schools. In 1917, the American federal government passed the Smith-Hughes Act which provided funding for a national system of vocational education administered through a separate Federal Board. It was the first and most important piece of federal legislation in the field of vocational education and its major provisions remained untouched for almost half a century.

The Cult of Efficiency

Raymond Callahan once described the movement toward a scientific measurement of educational failures or successes as the "Great Panacea," using the dollar as a single evaluative criterion. According to Callahan, the prelude of time leading to the passing of the Smith-Hughes Act was also the period in which America discovered the efficiency expert. In a sudden flood of enthusiasm with the notion, an attempt was made to apply the principles of scientific management to other aspects of American life. Of course, the school immediately became a target, and in 1911 a group of seven administrators was appointed to a committee on the economy of time in education. The name of Frederick W. Taylor vaulted into prominence via his book, *Principles of Scientific Management,* which was translated into many foreign languages giving sure indication that the concern for efficiency was not merely a North American phenomenon.

It was Frank Spaulding, a superintendent of schools in Passaic, New Jersey, who popularized both the language and concept of efficiency, equating the education of children to such physical and technical tasks as laying bricks, mining pig iron or cutting metals. The data on which he expected to base the measurement of a school's efficiency would include the percentage of children of each year of age in a respective school district, the average number of days attended for each child, the average length of time required for each child to master a simple concept or unit of work, and the percentage of children who actually completed a certain number of units. Ultimately Spaulding could come up with figures which indicated that a pupil recitation in English could cost 7.2 cents in a vocational school while it costs only five cents in a technical school. "Why are we paying a higher percentage of cost for the same skills in vocational schools than we do in technical schools?" he wanted to know.

While classicists generally ignored these kinds of analyses and promulgations, since they had nothing to do with real education anyway, the progressivists were appalled at the arrogance of relegating human tasks to the cognitive junk-heap of scrap metals and coal mines. The human mind was deserving of more respect than that, they claimed, and accused the promoters of efficiency of disregarding individuality and creativity and ignoring the reality of individual perception.

Taylor and Spaulding's principles of efficiency found ready support in the work of Edward L. Thorndike, who developed a description of human learning in terms of the stimulus-response bond concept and tried to show that the process is the result of the organism (human being) responding to a series of stimuli. Thorndike identified a series of inherited tendencies such as reflexes and instincts, differentiating them from learned acts such as skill or complicated acts of thought. Learning then became a matter of strengthening and weakening the bonds between a situation present to sense and responses in the nervous system, and the status of the response agent (person). The correct responses could become fixed by exercise and the resulting satisfaction, while the unsuccessful responses might be dulled or eliminated by virtue of the dissatisfaction which they engendered. In actuality, Thorndike had to make allowances for circumstances in which the theory appeared not to work satisfactorily. A progressivist, Boyd Bode, criticized it as being nothing more than a combination of the principles of the laws of readiness, exercise and effect.

The blend of Thorndike's psychology and the cult of efficiency was quite functional in essence and objective. Thorndike once observed that education of the future would demand an increase in specialization and thus in the study of skills, habits, ideas and attitudes. He was no doubt prepared to project laws by which these could be attained and Spaulding was prepared to measure their attainment by students (or should we say, by organisms!). B. F. Skinner later carried on the behaviorist tradition by explaining away any concepts not previously dealt with by Thorndike. In analyzing human freedom, for example, Skinner could be accused of ignoring what had been said about existential freedom over the last one hundred years by writers such as Friedrich Nietsche, Soren Kierkegaarde, Martin Heidegger and Jean Paul Sartre, and elaborating a more "scientific" kind of concept, to wit; "Freedom is a matter of contingencies of reinforcement, not of the feelings the contingencies generate" (Bowers, 1974: 159).

The philosophical debate of the test-oriented followers of Thorndike with the progressivists continues to this day albeit in somewhat less headline grabbing ways. Among many educators there is a "both are right" attitude that prevails and gives evidence either to the fact of ignorance that prevails in that constituency, or to the possibility that philosophical consistency is either an unknown or devalued commodity today.

Science Rules

In the fall of 1957 the Russians launched the world's first mechanical satellite into orbit and the American scientific community went wild! Why were the Russians the first to accomplish this feat? Perhaps it was . . . yes indeed, it was because the schools had gone soft on learning and students were incapable of excelling in the arena of scientific accomplishment. Progressivist ideas were blamed for watering down content and the classicists were slammed for emphasizing irrelevant ideas. Ivan could read and Johnny could not. Public education had become a wasteland of "experience-centred nothingness."

Chief among the critics was the German-educated missile expert, Werner von Braun, who later guided the American foray into space. He was accompanied by Admiral Hyman Rickover (1960), father of the nuclear-submarine program. It was almost comical to witness how quickly public funds could be allocated for "scientific" programs involving education from elementary through university levels. Anything even smacking of science was funded;

teachers flocked to scholarship-sponsored summer schools and enrolled in a wide variety of institutes for course-work that would allegedly improve America's scientific orientation and expertise (Fain et al., 1979).

Putting the situation bluntly, critic Rickover (1960) charged that America was militarily weak and growing increasingly dependent on other nations who were becoming the "sinews of our economic and military power." He found it paradoxical that Soviet engineers could do highly competent work despite authoritarian control and attributed their success to a contradiction in the Russian system. Apparently, they allowed some of their superior personalities special "capitalist-like" privileges. For America, the solution lay with the schools. Too many children were "enjoying school" but not getting the kind of education that the twentieth century required.

Part of the solution to the dilemma described by Rickover came in the form of the Conant Report. In the preface to the report, John W. Gardner, a strong Rickover supporter, commended Conant for his fresh look at the American education system, denied that Conant had been influenced by the Sputnik happening and encouraged Americans to accept Conant's challenge that any school could become a good school if his recommendations for comprehensive high schools were implemented. Truly, this would produce an educational system with something for everyone.

The presses that hurriedly ground out several editions of Conant's Report had hardly cooled when the decade of the sixties began. It was a time of intrigue in American educational history, as many can still recall, and initiated a series of alternative solutions, some of which were not even remotely connected to the three major streams of traditionalism, progressivism or vocationalism.

Philosophically Unanchored in the 21st Century

Although the quest for a new approach to pedagogy has become grounded in philosophical mire, the new kid on the block (at least as a slogan) has been labelled "constructivism." Built on the foundation of progressivism, advocates for contemporary school reform insist that any plans to change schools, even philosophically, should involve the entire community. Constituents, they argue, should be able to buy-in to the operation instead of being given the impression that schools belong to the professionals. Constructivists are very concerned about school reform and believe that the success of a genuine school improvement effort requires selecting and maintaining a clear, long-term focus on a few important priorities. All players should be consulted in formulating these goals and they should all be involved at each stage of development. As Wagner (1998: 516) states, "All school improvement plans should be public documents and should be widely read and discussed both within and beyond the schools."

Not all constituents will be comfortable with the constructivist approach, particularly those within the professional stronghold itself. Recently a few schools in Boston decided to implement a system of peer review which resulted in school principals being reviewed by their peers. Wagner (1998) notes that the final drafts of the reviews were consistently of higher quality than those released by central office personnel. The next step was to incept a "bottom up" kind of review that would involve an even larger constituency. The fundamental key to this approach was that collaboration is better than compliance.

The philosophical underpinnings of constructivism are essentially pragmatic in nature, namely that knowledge exists in the minds of people only and is constructed from within, in interrelation with the world. The meanings which people assign to phenomena depend on their previous experiences. Thus knowledge is constructed through perception and action. The good news is that there is a vat of common knowledge "out there" that derives from a common brain and body which are part of the same universe. In terms of educational application, this means that fundamentally teachers and students can share the same perceptual knowledge which forms the basis of school curricula. Granted the perceptions of young students may not be as "accurate" as those of trained scientists, but since they will be functioning according to those perceptions theirs may be deemed an equally valid form of knowledge. In order for those perceptions to constitute a fuller comprehension of reality, it is suggested that teachers encourage students to discuss, explain, or evaluate, their ideas and procedures (Hendry, 1996). The objective is that in such a milieu, all participants may come to a fuller knowledge of "the truth."

Another recent arrival on the philosophical scene has been labelled postmodernism, but the name poses a difficulty with somewhat presumptuous implications. Modernity is generally defined as the historical period between the Renaissance and the late twentieth century, a time during which western society shifted from an agrarian model to a democratic industrial society (Wells et al., 1999). Since we are now edging out of the modern period, postmodernism may be conceived of as representing all thoughts that occur after modern times are over. Thus philosophy will have been labelled for all time. Everything after modern times may legitimately be called postmodern. The presumptuous title notwithstanding, postmodernism appears to have nothing to offer that has not been better stated by pragmatists, relativists, Gestalt psychologists or existentialists. The major emphases of this perspective include impressionism (Johann Heinrich Pestalozzi), subjectivity (Jean Paul Sartre), and relativity (William James, Boyd Bode, Charles Sanders Peirce, and John Dewey). Even a little Gestalt occurs in the works when it is suggested that we need to move away from the apparent objectivity provided by third person narrators, fixed narrative points of view and clear-cut moral positions (Klages, 1997). Critics suggest that the phenomenon of charter schools embodies many of the contradictions of the so-called postmodern paradox. The major paradox of postmodernity is that the complexity and uncertainty wrought by globalization has led to a parallel search for meaning in locally defined identities (Wells et al., 1999). Fragmented and decentralized as they are, charter schools celebrate differences over uniformity and privatization over nationalism.

Spiro (1996) argues that the postmodernist critique of science consists of two interrelated arguments, epistemological and ideological. Both are based on subjectivity. First, human beings are subjective, and legitimate targets for anthropological study. According to the epistemological argument, anthropology cannot be a science since the subjective human arena comprises the principal subject area. Such a "science" is thus precluded from discovering objective truth. Since objectivity is an illusion, according to the ideological argument, so-called scientific truth will only subvert oppressed groups, females, ethnics and third world peoples. Postmodernism is essentially an eclectic movement with special interest in aesthetics, architecture and philosophy with only limited relevance for education. Its denial of any form of universal truth and reason disallows the development of any standardized curriculum since it would not address special needs induced by gender, race or social class. Kanpol (1992) suggests that it might be useful to fall back and at least try to establish workable truths for each social sector. Without such a framework the postmodernist stance will have only limited value in a democracy. This would mean that postmodernism will amount to little more than just another short-lived social movement. Its emergence, however, speaks clearly to the philosophical hodgepodge of the contemporary educational enterprise and suggests why the fragmentation of public schooling is so readily being welcomed. John Dewey must be turning over in his grave.

Four
Private and Parochial Schools:
The Traditional Alternative

Before the concept of the common school originated, and even as it was being developed, the logical or even preferred way to educate one's children was via private or parochial schools. Denominational schools still comprise the most financed form of private or parochial education, particularly in the United States, but several Canadian provinces also operate separate Roman Catholic or Protestant school districts. The earliest established universities, although denominationally linked, were also financed by the state. After the US War of Independence in 1776, this situation persisted, and if it had not been for the First Amendment to the US Constitution, the American federal government might even have considered establishing a national church (McClendon, 1966: 311). By 1840, however, the handwriting was on the wall, and the power of state churches began to wane. Increasing immigration was also a factor because arriving peoples brought with them their own forms of belief and worship which did not always augur well with the Christian-oriented perspective of the founding fathers. There were also schisms within established denominations in America which made the educational situation more complex.

Denominationally-sponsored schools in the United States gradually became nonsectarian, and religious leaders set about establishing alternative forms of educating their children. In the 1840s the Presbyterian Church urged its congregations to establish schools for children aged five to twelve, and for some years the project flourished. A similar attempt by the Lutheran Church (Missouri Synod), fared better and soon the Lutherans had in operation the largest Protestant school system in the United States. Before long the Roman Catholic Church followed suit, largely motivated by the many Irish and German Catholic immigrants who came to America. In 1884 the Roman Catholic Church made it mandatory for each parish to sponsor a local school.

Private schools have traditionally featured such characteristics as separation of the sexes, school uniforms, academic excellence as an aim, and a limiting selection process. For the most part, proponents of private schools like to point out that these institutions have produced what they have claimed, namely, students with higher than average achievement and a mastery of subject matter supplementary to state or provincial requirements (Glatthorn, 1975). As the development of tax-based education gained ground in North America, the promoters of private schools agitated for public tax support which was eventually granted, although at first only on a limited basis.

Origins of Public Schooling

The original plan of the American colonial government was to make public schooling available to all. This objective was soon averted by higher status citizen groups who did not relish the idea of their children attending school with people of lower socio-economic backgrounds. Some school founders could not conceive of a system that was not fundamentally religious and therefore developed parochial schools. Parochial school systems have not only survived in America, some of them have thrived. Based on the assumption that denominational purity must be maintained, however, these schools have injected a hearty dose of both religious and cultural ethnocentrism into their curricular ongoings. Originally begun by religious groups with strong nationalistic loyalties, efforts have been made by religious educators to teach the young about the beauties of the "old country" and gain an appreciation for what their forebears had to suffer in order for them to enjoy the freedom available in America. McClendon has (1966) pointed out that the Irish in particular developed a series of institutional devices for maintaining their religious loyalties in an environment that had become hostile to them. Moreover, their cultural maintenance was assured by the fact that each group who immigrated to the United States brought with them a core of religious personnel.

A similar situation prevailed among German Lutherans whose commitment to transported cultural modes was strengthened by their extensive use of the German language. Only when antagonism against German-speaking groups rose during the Second World War did Lutheran schools become bilingual. Of the fourteen million Americans who spoke a foreign tongue as a first language in America in the 1940s, three and one quarter million spoke German. Like their Irish and Italian counterparts, the German Lutherans gave credibility to the meaning of the word parochial as separate, narrow and provincial.

As public schools gradually began to represent the primary mode for educating children, interest in private schooling did not necessarily wane. Cultural maintenance via schooling was prized highly by many incoming groups. There were also those who became disillusioned with facets of public schooling and started private schools as a means of rectifying what they perceived to be shortcomings. The failure of the public school to meet the demands for religious and moral instruction was a primary concern. On the whole, parents casting about for superior educational facilities sometimes joined forces with those seeking cultural protection and thus developed alternative private institutions. Some of these schools became quite famous for their successful experimentation with and development of new methods and materials of instruction (Brubacher, 1966).

The Roman Catholic Experience

Easily the most extensive of parochial school systems in America today is operated by the Roman Catholic Church. Archbishop John Hughes (1797-1864) of New York first tried to influence the public school system to acknowledge Catholic beliefs and values in school ongoings, but to no avail. This led him to apply for public funds to subsidize Catholic parochial schools but after controversy erupted, he was rejected. The State of New York decided to fund only one public school system and did so by legislative act in 1842. President Ulysses S. Grant publicly endorsed the position, and America gave birth to one completely publicly funded school system.

A subtle, yet successful alternative devised by the Catholic Church was developed at Poughkeepsie, New York, in which one public school was set up with the added feature of offering religious instruction in the Catholic faith in the half hour before the school officially opened. The chosen site was actually a building owned by the Catholic Church, and many of the staff were members of the church. The school was publicly funded, and used the curriculum, texts and methods of the public system. Moreover, it was always open to inspection by public authorities. Although the plan worked well for two decades in a number of communities, it was eventually judged insufficient by Roman Catholic authorities. Subsequently, their energies were devoted towards the establishment of a full-fledged alternative system of their own.

Today's Roman Catholic parochial school system operates according to a synthesized philosophy of education. It is the Catholic view that the school should support and extend what is taught by the home and by the church. This does not mean that the single purpose of schooling is specific religious indoctrination, for the school also has the obligation to provide an education that is useful for both time and eternity. Catholic schools attempt to provide all needed skills and aptitudes required at all levels. This includes emphasis on spiritual development, a facet that cannot presently be accommodated in public schools. For this reason Catholics have been fervent in their drive to provide an wholistic education for their children. As Pope Pius XI stated (Gross 1962: 130-131):

> Christian education takes in the whole aggregate of human life, physical and spiritual, intellectual and moral, individual, domestic and social, not with a view of reducing it in any way, but in order to ele-

vate and perfect it, in accordance with the example and teaching of Christ.

The success of parochial schools is partially based on the intimate connection between the cultural background of the sponsoring group and their success in establishing and maintaining a mass educational enterprise. This is particularly true of the larger systems maintained by Roman Catholics and Lutherans. Early in the history of the American Roman Catholic Church, the parochial system even became a kind of symbol of the integrity of the church.

Parochial schools tend to serve as an important institutional device for religious rather than cultural maintenance. About 85 percent of children attending private (parochial) schools in the United States are enrolled in Roman Catholic Schools. The various synods of Lutheran Churches enroll about a quarter of a million students in over 2 500 private schools (Cooper, 1988: 22).

Despite the growth and success of parochial education, in a study conducted in New England, Rossi and Rossi (1968) found that there was very little difference between parochial schooled Catholics and other Catholics. The influence of the Catholic school was most dramatically shown in areas where the church has traditionally taken a strong stand, namely in support for religious education or on the performance of ritual duties. Other areas showed parochially-schooled Catholics to be only marginally different from other Catholics. This led them to conclude that the best intent of parochial schools was carried out in religious terms and these schools did not appear to be a major mechanism by which Catholics maintained themselves as a distinct grouping in America. What the schools did accomplish as a corollary objective was to serve as a recruiting front for the priesthood and lay church staff.

Recruitment aside there is evidence to suggest that Roman Catholic schools are academically efficient. Madsen (1996: 17) discusses the results of a study that tracked Roman Catholic high schools students in their second year through graduation. It was discovered that these students had a higher achievement level than their public school counterparts. The researchers controlled for socio-economic background and differing levels of achievement and still found that Roman Catholic students increased their achievements by one grade level.

The Canadian Scene

Formal education in Canada is basically a provincial matter so that there are ten quite distinct provincial systems rather than one in the country. The British North America Act (BNA) of 1867 guaranteed educational jurisdiction to the provinces and this was affirmed by the Canadian Constitution Act of 1982. Provincial departments of education can mandate a great deal of the responsibility for operating schools on a day-to-day basis to local levels in which case responsibility is handled by elected school boards. Private schools receive a little support for their operation from provincial authorities and the amount of support varies from one province to another. In the meantime, parents who elect to send their children to private schools must still pay taxes to either of the two school systems, public or separate.

The BNA Act allowed for the establishment of two systems of education in Canada and certain provinces have allowed for both kinds of schools to operate (Giles and Proudfoot, 1984). Generally speaking, these systems have informally come to be known as the public and Roman Catholic (separate) systems. One unique exception exists in St. Albert, Alberta where the separate school system is Protestant in identity and the public system is Roman Catholic. As previously indicated, a unique school system combining religion and education was formed and operated in Newfoundland until the mid-1990s. All public schools in that province operated as denominational systems and were governed by Anglican, Roman Catholic, Pentecostal, Salvation Army and United Church denominations. The provincial government eventually wearied of this arrangement and in September, 1995, held a provincial referendum on control of schooling. The citizens of Newfoundland by a slight majority decided that the province's schools should become truly public and governed by local school boards. Although these reforms are gradually being put into place, leaders of the religious denominations are hard at work to maintain their historical right to operate Newfoundland's schools and compromises are constantly being made.

Canada's history of private schooling is closely linked to both religion and elitism (Lupul, 1970). Until about a half century ago private schools in Canada could be regarded as somewhat of an anomaly since they were basically designed for boys, operated as instruments of privilege and afforded status ascription to those who frequented their halls (Weinzweig, 1977). The number of private schools has risen in Canada over the last decade, and most of these schools have been begun by religious organizations. Private schools in Canada receive very little government funding and often operate with very strong constituency support both in terms of finances as well as emotionally. Unlike their predecessors, which featured selective recruitment, boundary maintenance, containment and impermeability, today's private schools often attempt to attract students from a much wider constituency, primarily because of financial need. Despite these challenges, enrollment in private schools is growing in Canada.

Alternative Schools in Canada

Although private schools in North America are almost as old as the nations of Canada and the United States, the idea of alternative schooling "within the public system" is of fairly recent origins. Today the emphasis on alternative forms of educating primarily brings to mind either charter schools or home schooling. A more rare form of alternative education would be Logos (religious) schools, which used to operate in Calgary, Alberta and which currently are being proposed in various cities in western Canada.

Gagné (1996) suggests that alternative schools designed to stream students into either high or low achievement environments tend to put some students at a disadvantage. Research supports this claim, providing evidence of a lack of mobility of students between the various levels of school streams. There is a pronounced shift downwards in academic achievement as students who are not achieving to the satisfaction of school officials are encouraged to enroll in less academically challenged courses. Data gathered in the Province of Ontario, for example, indicates that students in lower-stream classes drop out much more readily than their counterparts in more academically-oriented streams (Gagné, 1996).

The alternative school concept per se is a tiring and with rare exceptions diminishing concept in Canada. The initial idea was to make available a bona fide form of schooling with a specific emphasis within a regularly established system, usually motivated by religious sources, although there were also exceptions. A decade ago many public school systems featured a degree of variety within their ranks. The Calgary public system, for example, included the Plains Indians Cultural Survival School (PICSS), two Logos (Christian) Schools, two Hebrew Schools and an Alternative High School, and this pattern was not unique. Other cities featured similar developments. Today, only two of these schools remain in the Calgary system, namely PICSS and the Alternative High School. Contact School, an alternative high school in Toronto, has also successfully survived recent changes in school structure and still manages to assist at-risk youth in restoring their interests in studying (Gagné, 1996).

Private schools in Canada are subject to a fairly standard series of regulations in the various provinces in which they operate, but still have to depend on the procurement of extra fees in order to operate. In most cases they follow provincial curricula, employ certified teachers and seek to fulfil a series of educational objectives closely akin to those of the public system. Deviations include an extraordinary stress on academic excellence or religious goals. Private school enrollments climbed steadily over the decades of the 1970s and 1980s reaching a total of 4.5 percent of the nation's children by 1990 (Bergen, 1990). Financial assistance to these schools is both varied and limited across the provinces, and there is no guarantee that current levels of support will continue. Lobbyists for enhanced support have recently collided with hard-nosed politicians bent on making severe educational cutbacks that will affect every sector of schooling as we know it.

Public Versus Private Schools

Defending Private Schools

Literature on the private versus public schools debate has mounted in recent years. Public system supporters in the United States, for example, survived their most severe blow in 1966 when the infamous study by James S. Coleman was released. Leaning strongly toward the side of private schools, Coleman left no stone unturned in his quest to settle the argument once and for all by relying on the results of extensive social science research. A few years later a follow-up study was undertaken and many people worried that Coleman would again defend the record of private schools and encourage means of financing them from the public purse via tuition tax credits and vouchers. All of this would serve to undermine public education (Coleman, 1982). Coleman did conclude that private schools (specifically Catholic parochial schools) did more nearly approximate the American ideal, but he shied away from making policy recommendations that would encourage further development of the private system (Ravitch, 1981).

One of the findings of Coleman's research pertained to the claim that school achievement was not necessarily related to forms of schooling as much as to school policy. Coleman contended that private schools were not any better than public schools but they did place greater emphasis on higher rates of academic engagement. School attendance was more consistent, and students did extra homework. One other important difference pertained to curricular tracking. Only thirty-four percent of public school students enrolled in academic curricula, while thirty-nine percent enrolled in a general curriculum, and twenty-seven percent took the vocational route. By contrast, seventy percent of private school students were enrolled in an academic program, twenty-one percent in a general course and only nine percent in vocational. Thus the dominant school emphasis basically determined academic choices and successes of students.

A recent study of 3 374 high school graduates by Lee and colleagues (1998) confirms this finding. These researchers compared scores of high school graduates from public, Roman Catholic and private schools with the High School Effectiveness Supplement to the National Education Longitudinal Study of 1988 and concluded that students in private schools took more courses in mathematics, and Catholic schools tried strongly to influence their students' course-taking behaviors. It also became obvious that while Catholic schools tended to enroll students whose demographic and academic backgrounds were similar to those of students in public schools, private schools tended to be more academically and economically selective.

Coleman did not report on the fact that private schools are generally out to prove something, being somewhat of a reactionary phenomenon, and therefore it would stand to reason that their promoters would strive to make them become centres of academic excellence. After all, if one is to spend the extra money getting one's offspring into a private school there must be good reasons for it. Evidently these parents would also think that academic achievement is related to economic success and they want the "best" for their children. There is also the societal reality that somehow academic achievement is superior to any other school objective regardless of whether or not students can achieve academically.

Although one of the more frequently raised claims for privatizing schooling is that these schools are more academically successful, there are also many ways in which private schools can be quite atypical. Often students from higher income families gravitate to private schools, mainly because their parents are able to afford it. Staff members at these schools often take unusual pride in their work to the extent that they exhude an intensified degree of professional integrity and independence. Private school proponents claim to provide these features: superior physical and social environment; a manageable plant and system size; programs that are tailored to the needs of the students, staff and constituency; a moral emphasis or at least a "value-centred" curriculum; and, mutually satisfactory peer-group contacts (Bergen, 1982). In contrast to most public schools then, one would have to conclude that private schools sometimes offer unique advantages.

Criticism of Private Schools

A few critics of private schools mince no words in their opposition to private schools. Laurier LaPierre, for example, stated that private schools breed snobs, are instruments for abusing children, and are more concerned about the parental image than children's welfare (*Calgary Herald,* Sept. 24, 1983). LaPierre had completed a two-year study on schooling when he made his observations and based his remarks on the assumption that while public education has been unduly harshly criticized, private education has been allowed to get away with unorthodox activities.

There is evidence of another kind. A study (Paterson, 2000) of anti-Catholic bias in 23 social studies textbooks published by conservative Protestant groups indicated that such bias was identifiable and grew most intense as readers moved from lower to higher grade materials. Examples of bias included derogatory criticisms of the Roman Catholic Church, claims that followers of Romanism did not know that Christ died to save them from eternal judgment, and offering gratuitous detail regarding forms of persecution in describing historical instances of Catholic persecution of Protestants. The majority of these books were published by three companies: A Beka, School of Tomorrow and Bob Jones University. About 9 000 private schools purchase materials from A Beka alone.

The concern that private schools allegedly foster exclusivity either by catering to a special interest group or by emphasizing a particular philosophy of education which may be out of step with the value system of dominant society is valid. Generally speaking, liberal-minded educators will concur that diversity creates interest, but unbridled diversity raises some legitimate concerns. For instance, some critics have long argued that all educational organizations, including public and private schools, should be allowed to bid on an open competitive market for both clientele and financial resources (Erickson, 1979). The obvious problem is that there would be nothing to stop each educational institution from establishing entirely unique standards for curriculum and teaching credentials to the extent that radical differences might emerge. These differences might be easy to justify from a theoretical perspective, but the crunch could come if it were discovered that children from a few exceptional schools were cheated of literacy, warped by a values frame mitigating against equality for all citizens or shortchanged in some other pedagogical way.

A further criticism of private schools is that they cater to a select audience. The Labour Party in England in 1980 made this declaration (Walford, 1990: 38):

> Attendance at a private school means something far more than an education. In Britain it is the basic requirement for membership in the hierarchy which still dominates so many positions of power and influence. Private school fees therefore buy more than examination success. They are the admission charge for a ruling elite whose wealth gives them the power and the power gives them wealth.

Levin (1989) has tackled the claim made by supporters of private schools that these institutions are financially more efficient than public schools. Levin contends that most such comparisons have drastically underestimated the cost of private schools primarily by comparing only tuition costs. Catholic Schools, for example, often rely heavily on teaching clergy whose salaries understate substantially their market value. In addition, churches often utilize space for schools without charging the worth of that space as an operational expense. When private schools costs are compared with public schools the mandated extras that the latter must provide are also often overlooked. For example, public schools must conform to more rigorous standards when it comes to providing facilities for needy students such as the disabled. The same requirement applies to vocational education which again requires the provision of additional facilities.

Madsen (1996: 13) argues that increased competitiveness, which is often inspired by the growth of private schools, can be a debilitating characteristic. Instead of enhancing academic achievement and "bringing out the best in everybody," competitiveness between students contributes to the development of a hierarchical system. In a competitive market, schools already advantaged will have substantial leverage over poorer, less developed schools. Based on this argument, if the state should choose to deregulate public education it would be shrinking its responsibility for providing quality education for all its students. As Madsen notes, competition creates inequality because those with financial resources can leave a school if they are dissatisfied with its operation or delivery, while those who are poor are trapped in ineffective schools.

The argument that parents who send their children to private schools are being unfairly double-taxed is fallacious. It is true that all citizens must pay school tax to a public system even if their children do not use their services, but this is the price of choice. The same argument can be applied to the utilization of any other public or private institutional offering. If people choose to go to a free public park they have the same opportunity as any other citizen. If individuals choose to frequent a private park that charges a fee, however, this is up to the citizen. If he or she deems it worthwhile or more enjoyable to utilize a private park instead of a public park, he or she must expect to pay for its use. Only public parks, sponsored by public taxation, can be free to all citizens. The only way to avoid "double-taxation" in such a circumstance is not to provide any services publicly and collectively if it is possible to provide it privately, a position which few would defend (Breneman, 1983).

When the student roster of some private schools is examined, it will be discovered that the characteristics of students are somewhat atypical. A.S. Neill's Summerhill, for example, often drew students who had difficulties in regular public schools. The St. John's Boys Schools in Canada, operated by the Company of the Cross in the Anglican Church, are sometimes seen as boot-camps of sorts featuring rigorous physical requirements and strict discipline policies. Their students, too, are often problem students whose parents feel their children need a more rigorous environment in which to become motivated. There are also ivy league private schools whose students are anything but typical in the sense of representing a cross-section of society. These students tend to form a unique group in that they all have rich parents whose values represent only a small fraction of well-to-do citizenry. In that sense they are very atypical.

In Canada, private schools have had a foot in public territory for some years, and this will likely continue. The concept of alternative schools within public systems has only been the subject of experimentation, and is even now being replaced by other forms. The new arrival on the scene is the "charter school" which is basically a specialized, privately-run school with full government per-student funding. Charter schools are allegedly open to all students who can benefit from the program offered. School officials solicit students by advertising a special program and each school is incorporated as a society. Charter schools cannot charge tuition fees, they must be non-sectarian and they must employ certified teachers. The curriculum may be chosen by parents and school operators and must be subject to provincial approval as to standards and testing. These schools are being introduced in Canada on an experimental basis and, if nothing else, will comprise yet another potential educational research population.

Analysis

A study in Britain (Walford, 1990) reveals that parents largely select private schools for several basic reasons. About a third of parents surveyed sent their children to private schools simply because it was a family tradition or because "it was the best thing to do" (Walford, 1990: 42). More specifically, twenty-eight percent claimed that attendance at a private school would enable their children to "get on better in life," while twenty-three percent believed that such schools offered greater academic advantage. A further fourteen percent insisted that such schools would develop character and foster discipline. After examining the data pertaining to these claims, Walford discovered that some of the better schools did indeed deliver on the parental hope for greater academic achievement, but they were probably less effective in terms of ensuring that their graduates would "get on" in their chosen careers (Walford, 1990: 60). While these students performed admirably in school, this was no guarantee that they would be successful in their chosen careers.

Perhaps the most often-made claim for superiority by private school supporters has to do with academic achievement. While studies are available to support that claim, the conclusion must be stacked against the reality that parents who aspire to higher achievement on the part of their offspring, tend to choose private schools for that very reason. In that sense the results constitute a self-fulfilling prophecy.

A variation of the public versus private arrangement has been to contract out support services in public schools. In smaller school divisions this has proven to be financially feasible since smaller systems cannot always provide for all needed support services. By contracting to provide support services to school districts, particularly those located in close proximity to each other, private entities can often provide services at lower costs than the districts could themselves. The disadvantages of such a plan, however, is that once in motion they may grow to take over elements of the school program which are better left in the public domain. The plan has political overtones depending on who is awarded the contracts. It also means decreased managerial control for the school and because of the potential for improprieties, could result in diminished reliability or quality of service (Lyons, 1995).

An interesting phenomenon in China is the recent growth spurt of private schools albeit for quite unique reasons (Kwong, 1997). Private schools in China emerged in the 1980s in response to the shortage of schools, the Chinese government either not being willing or able to provide schooling for the country's population. A great diversity exists in these schools for the elite; there are primary and junior-senior high schools, vocational schools and university preparation schools. All private schools are profit-making, and educational expectations vary. Elite private schools will likely establish a new hierarchy in China's educational system, while educational expectations for ordinary private schools are low (Lin, 1994). Facilities consist of a chalkboard, a desk and a chair for each student. Curriculum offerings in these schools vary, offering instruction in such fields as tailoring, typing, cosmetology, electronics or vehicle repair. In 1997 there were 960 653 private schools operating in China providing schooling for four percent of the population.

The Equality Factor

Much of the controversy over the Coleman Report dealt with such matters as integration, Coleman himself mandating that lower socio-economic African American children be mixed with middle class whites to provide stronger motivation for achievement. Despite this thrust Coleman was of the opinion that public schools – or the process of education itself –were not the social equalizers American society imagined them to be. School achievement was found to be more closely related to family background and socio-economic class and these variables would be more difficult to change. Educators who analyzed the Coleman Report discovered that Coleman may have been right all along. Students who performed best on achievement tests were often enrolled in the same schools as those who performed worst (Bell, 1973). Perhaps integration was a valid form of reform after all.

Crain and Rossell (1989) found that private schools often constitute a safe haven for AngloAmerican students who flee from desegregation. While many research studies on the subject make no distinction between flight to private schools and residential relocation, these authors discovered significantly less residential relocation than private school enrollment in most school districts in response to school desegregation. They also found that the

primary criterion in avoiding desegregation was money; whites tended to cal-
culate the costs and benefits of their actions and chose the course of action
with the lowest costs. In comparing enrollment figures, Catterall and Levin
(1982) found that minority group enrollments in private schools was quite
low. In one survey it was found that African American children accounted for
fourteen percent of public high school enrollments and only six percent of
private school enrollments. Coleman (1982) found that families of students
in private secondary schools had an annual income of $23 200, compared
with $18 700 for families of public secondary school students.

Private schools have the luxury of turning away students they don't
want, which is a rarity in public schools. Brown (1995: 115) states;

> Education is a public good. Schools are designed not only to educate
> children but also to promote racial, gender and social class equity. In a
> true private market system, you would fire or get rid of low producers,
> but in education you cannot get rid of low-productive students.

A public school teacher in Calgary offered a similar sentiment; "we have to
take everyone in our schools; they (private schools) can choose who they
want to take." Unfortunately this can also be the case in private schools but
often for the wrong reasons. When private schools experience financial difficulties, they are quite apt to "lower their standards" and admit students with
a wider range of backgrounds and academic abilities.

It appears evident that the choice for private schooling is usually based
on the superior academic success which these schools lay claim to. This,
however, is not the whole picture. Some parents simply choose a school on
the basis of the students and their families who support a particular school.
Madsen (1996: 15) points out that some parents choose certain private
schools on the basis of racial affiliation. In one study reported by Madsen it
was discovered that African American children chose a particular school
because there were more African American students enrolled, even though
they knew that another school they could go to had fewer African American
students enrolled with better academic records. Parents of those students felt
mildly perturbed about their children's choice, but they deferred to them.

Private school supporters contend that since their schools are often
smaller they permit the development of a strong sense of community which
public schools generally lack. In a private school everyone supports the mission of the school through extra-curricular programs and increased parental
involvement. These schools have well-defined boundaries and administrators
and staff work hard to promote a sense of ownership on behalf of the school
constituency. When unduly extended, however, these campaigns can backfire
and, in fact, create the very sense of exclusivity for which critics castigate
them. In all fairness, there are many public schools which have very successfully created a sense of community within their constituency, particular-

ly rural schools and smaller urban schools. One of the most powerful factors in developing school pride, public or private, is a strong sports program and its success in gaining community support is strictly up to the energies exerted in this regard by school administration and staff.

On the negative side is the reality that not everyone in a small community is honor-bound to uphold the reputation of the clan. As Bosetti (2000: 187) notes, the strong connection between private or charter school and local community can also have its downside. The school may be subject to repercussions of conflict among community members and the governing body. The example given by Bosetti pertains to an Arabic charter school in Alberta in which strong disagreements arose about the language employed. Arabic-speaking parents, who were loyal to their language, spoke it exclusively to their children and to Arabic-speaking teachers in the school. The others began to resent this form of what they perceived as exclusivity with the result that the Arabic-speaking students began to feel marginalized and experienced difficultly maintaining respect from other students and their parents.

Doyle (1982) noted two decades ago that private schooling was on the rise in North America although the reasons for its growth were unclear. Later, the efforts of Presidents Ronald Reagan and George Bush further encouraged the privatization of public education. The movement began as a political tool to promote an alternative that would impede further federal interventions to implement *Brown* by bussing children to racially integrate public schools. The United States government then offered support for magnet school programs (choice in public schools), and the alternatives later evolved into a movement for privatization of public education supported by government vouchers. There was also an effort to encourage improved management and more efficiency by introducing "market" competition into the public school improvement equation (Brown, 1995). In January, 2001, President George W. Bush made a public statement that he was backing off from giving strong support to a school voucher plan and instead concentrating on inaugerating a national school testing plan *(U.S. News & World Report*, February 5, 2001: 19). He stressed the idea that the standards of academic achievement for high school graduates must be raised to equip people for the jobs in this information age. In addition, rigorous annual testing would be installed for grades three to eight to make sure that no one was falling behind. School officials were to be held personally responsible for student achievement with rewards for successful educators and penalties for educators whose students did not do well *(Akron Beacon Journal*, May 6, 2001).

The historic peak for private schools in the United States was in 1971 when 51 271 000 students were enrolled. Over the next fifteen years the total number of students declined by twelve percent and then moved back upwards (MacEwan, 1996: 6). In Canada the scene was a bit different. After the early 1970s and until the mid 1990s student enrollments in private elementary and high schools in Canada nearly doubled while enrollments in public schools dipped slightly.

In so far that there is a positive side to the argument, private schools often attract families with more financial means who have higher expectations for their children. As a result, staff members may also take special pride in their work because of the constituency they are seeking to impress. Private schools are usually smaller, and therefore have a much more manageable plant to care for, they can make more rules to protect their interests and they can tailor programs to better fit the smaller size of their student body. Bergen (1982) suggested that private schools appeal to students with special needs because public schools are simply not able to provide for the unique educational needs of some students. He insisted that private schools could be much more amendable because of their smaller size and greater interest in pleasing their constituents. He recommended that public school systems not try to compete with private schools but rather augur for departments of education to work out appropriate controls for their operation and have public school officials seek symbiotic relationships with them.

The growth of private schooling and increased involvement by non-governmental organizations in education suggests serious implications for public schools. Advocates for private schools usually stress two important advantages to their existence, the *first* being that they offer choice to parents who want something different (or what they perceive as better) for their children. They argue that it is a human right to be able to select a specific learning environment for one's offspring. It is also good for schools to participate in the free market place. A *second* argument is that public schools simply cannot offer the full range of options that become available when private schools are added to the roster of choices. Now it is possible that what they are really saying is that their own preferences and values must be accommodated, not necessarily those of their children. Now that charter schools are a reality, however, with their offerings of a whole plethora of teaching and learning styles, this argument loses much of its punch.

According to Finn (1982) the resolution of the public versus private argument will have to deal with five realities, the *first* of which is funding. As governments continue to struggle to deal with the cutbacks of the 1980s, additional restrictions on funding for special projects like private schools are still under severe scrutiny. A *second* reality is the world of alternative education which includes private/parochial and charter schools as well as home schooling. These alternatives do not represent a unified community. Ideally, one should be able to conceive of the public system versus the "other" system, but this is not the case. In many instances the constituents represented by alternative camps is a mixture of strange bedfellows. Often these systems reflect a greater degree of mistrust for one another than they have for the public system. It also helps to keep in mind that many of the inventors of these systems are products of public schools themselves. As such, they probably reflect a degree of dissatisfaction, distrust or rebellion against the system which they are attempting to replace. This does not necessarily make for a healthy outlook for one's offspring.

A *third* reality identified by Finn is that public school supporters tend to be suspicious of alternative education, perhaps because they are too often attacked and they perceive that the innovators have a hidden or anti-societal agenda. It could simply be a called of "fear of the unknown," but more than likely these suspicions emanate from personal resentment; "Why do they feel that our system is not good enough?" *Fourth*, Finn contends that private schools have never enjoyed the support of the America's top elite who often sent their children abroad for education. If they had such support, private schools might be an even greater threat to public education.

The *fifth* and final reality is that today private and parochial school systems are generally doing well. The growth of charter schools is a new phenomenon, and may possibly pose an even greater challenge for public schooling. Governments that support charter schools may see their increase as a means of dismantling any power structure that public school teachers and officials may have. As this trend continues, the financial base of public education may also be weakened. If charter schools continue to maintain their hold on public funding, almost anything can happen. Their success may bolster private arguments for equal funding, or charter schools may even transform themselves into a series of private schools.

There is no question that private and charter schools pose a challenge to public schools to get their act together. As the world continues to shrink, however, it will be necessary for these alternative systems to branch out and contemplate if not participate in global as well as national realities.

Need for Public Schools

Current arguments for additional funding for nonpublic schooling is hinged on the principle that parents should have the freedom to choose for their children, as long as their schooling arrangement is subject to periodic inspection, an approved curriculum is utilized and certified teachers are hired. This is fine as far as it goes, but when private schools are allowed to choose whom they want to enroll, the democratic principle of equality is bypassed. The appropriate concern about private education has to do with the exclusivity which they foster either by catering to a special interest group or by emphasizing a philosophy of education which may be a little out of step with public values. Some proponents of private education make a strong case for diversity which they claim is part and parcel of any democratic society; as such, private and public schools should be allowed to bid for clientele on an equal basis (Erickson, 1979). An obvious problem with such an arrange-ment would be that there would be nothing to stop each educational institu-tion from establishing entirely unique standards for curriculum and teaching credentials so that radical differences might occur. While society may com-prise a democratic makeup, there is also the reality of trying to become a nation with national values and the guarantee of equal rights for all citizens. Surely, these deserve the attention which only a public system can provide.

It is a difficult challenge to guarantee equal rights for all citizens while trying to maintain some semblance of fair education for the nation's young. In answer to the question, "Do we need public schools in order to properly prepare future generations to live with a degree of ease as adults?" The answer has to be in the affirmative. Basic literacy can probably be furnished by any arrangement of schooling, but the opportunity to develop a global per-spective and rub shoulders with people representing all sectors of society is clearly only possible within the parameters of the public school.

The public school record is not without flaws. Research will show that there are always more adults who can read who have gone to school than those who have not, and there are always children attending some sort of school who will not learn to read. Generally speaking, children of literate parents learn to read even if they do not attend school. The reading diets of children whose parents are active in intellectual environments have a much more intense interest in books than children of parents who do not even read the daily news. When data on business and everyday math are examined, it will be discovered that society's illiterates all seem to be able to count, add and subtract sufficiently to get by even if they never went very far in school. Critics conclude that only a small percentage of people in a fully schooled society ever learn much more or need much more. Achievement tests in math indicate that only a few students do much better than chance in the formal structure of the subject. Students who are interested in math do much better than those who are not so motivated. It would be hard to prove that school-ing per se can even stimulate an added interest in the subject (Reimer, 1972).

Literacy is not the issue, however; values and outlook are. Children deserve to be able to do more than read. Public schools offer an environment in which their perspectives can broaden to include some knowledge of diver-gent value systems, world religions and economic systems. Johnson (1982) points out that public schools serve a preventative role in reducing society's ills via such subjects as vocational education, sex education, consumer edu-cation, etc. There are conditions to meet if this role is to prove effective, of course. One cannot simply make statements about random relationships between school attendance and literacy in defense of public schooling. It is also helpful to refer to a series of tested principles identified by Donovan (1983). First, we know that the more time spent in instructional situations, the greater the achievement attained, and the greater the amount of time spent with students by parents, the more likely they are to do better in school. On a corollary note, high expectations by school administrators may also be associated with higher achievement and the same is true of teachers. Better achievement is associated with a higher degree of structure and clear goals, and positive feedback also serves to motivate students to do better.

Even more convincing is evidence cited by Egerton (1982) who stated that for all of its flaws and shortcomings, the public school is the nearest thing we have to a publicly owned and operated social institution dedicated to the public good. It may not be popular to think of schooling as a social welfare agency, but it is that, and it needs to be. Preserving the public school is probably not the only way to provide equal opportunity or to assure equal access to learning for all echelons of society, but it is the best one we have. True, the media probably reaches nearly as many young minds as the school does, but it is never without some sort of economic or politically driven motive. The school is also a leavening agent; children meet here with their peers who represent nearly all steps on the national socio-economic ladder, and here they share with one another, complete lessons, and help form the next generation of society. According to Powell (1982: 11), "One of the best-kept secrets of American education is its historic commitment to serve 'average' children, a commitment which contradicts the usual images of high achievement and academic elitism in private schools." However, if the upward trend to support private schools continues, it will become increasingly difficult to maintain political support for public education. If the commitment to serve average children is to be fostered, and if the general social obligation of schooling is to be maintained, the question as to whether or not we need public schools is irrelevant. The question now becomes, "How will we be able to provide the best public education we can?"

Public schools have a full slate of social obligations to carry out including the fulfillment of such basic principles as democratic, universal, compulsory, practical and comprehensive education for all. How can this mandate be faithfully executed while rapid technological changes are foisting many nonessential adjustments in school ongoings – and this in the midst of a chorus of critics who, though they have been educated in that same institution, in every decade of the last century have lamented its inability to deliver.

If we are aware that these factors have positive results for students, and they are all available within the public school setting, the obvious question arises; "why would anyone want to dismantle a very workable and needed institution?"

Five
Redesigning Public Education in America: The Business Approach

By the middle of the 20th century the idea of universal public schooling was fairly well taken for granted in North America. Few parents, legislators or educators remembered with much fondness or appreciation how public education had evolved. Perhaps they were too engrossed in the other demands of modern life to pay much attention to muse about the challenges the venerable institution would face in the decades ahead. The right to being schooled was viewed in much the same way as other citizen privileges or guarantees of established values – democracy, personal choice, creativity and flexibility.

An examination of current educational trends suggests that the traditional format of the hallowed halls of public learning is being attacked in a manner not previously envisaged. The intensity of attack has not been witnessed since the formation of the institution. Although disinterested agitators for change have always played a role in seeking to revise the platform of any formalized version of the educational function, thankfully, many of their efforts have also gone awry. Strong defenders of the established system view any suggestion that significant changes need to be made to public education is viewed as tantamount to heresy. This is fundamentally true when the subject of diversity is brought up. It is useful to recall that the principle of diversity was entrenched in both the British North America Act, the forerunner of the Canadian Constitution, and the Constitution of the United States. Paradoxically, there has always been a conservative orientation towards education on this continent in that citizens have tended to restrain their enthusiasm for radical innovations until time has proven their worth. Granted this is much more a fact in Canada than in the United States, probably because Canadians are more conservative and a practical people who are more concerned that public schools should train for the job market, rather than develop the contemplative scholar. In contrast to their American counterparts, Canadians manifest a more limited degree of national consciousness and their concept of political socialization is evident only in terms of awareness of the formal political system, and perhaps disdain, not reverence for it.

The Quest For Diversity

Perhaps it was because of the great effort it took through the first half of the twentieth century to modernize public education, that by the 1950s most supporters of the system felt quite positive about their accomplishments. Although progressivist educators had hammered away at the traditionalist concept that there was something almost sacred about promoting the three R's as fundamental to the very concept of learning, the traditionalists prevailed. The formal organization which acted as the helm for many of the activities of the progressive education movement formally folded in the mid 1950s (Cremin, 1961). Clearly the most significant educational movement of this century, progressive education, caved in for a variety of reasons. By placing the interests, motivation and individual growth of the child at the forefront, the approach made inordinate demands on teachers' time and ability (Murphy, 1990). In one sense, by strenuously agitating for recognition of student individuality the movement's proponents personally took up the opportunity to develop individual approaches to reform, and so fostered dissent within the ranks. Sometimes it was even difficult for progressive educators to agree to disagree with dignity. Still, this "radical fringe" envisaged a new society which would be made possible through effective schooling and thus empower an additional generation of educators (Bowers, 1969). With the gradual emergence of a postwar conservativism in political and social thought progressive education came to a dismal end. The "back-to-the-basics" perspective prevailed.

Philosophical Concerns

The turbulent 1960s raised all kinds of questions about public schools and no doubt motivated the idea that greater diversity of both content and approach was needed in education. True, a number of innovative private schools were on the horizon, as were a few other challengers best grouped under the rubric of "free schools." The notion of alternative education per se, either as a new approach within the public system or without the system in the form of competitive institutions, primarily became the brainchild of the 1970s. Defenders of alternative education strongly rejected any notion that alternative schools threatened the public system, or that they should be viewed as interlopers to democratic education. They liked to point out that the necessity for alternative schools reflected very serious concerns about status quo education and the new alternative forms they proposed were not usually developed without some serious soul searching as well as financial considerations.

Basically, the premises on which the formation of alternative schools was posed were these:

(i) People learn in different ways, and different learning environments are essential both to meet the needs of individual students as well as to provide a choice for parents who want to assure maximum development on the part of their children.

(ii) Public schools are not always able to provide the particular emphasis (religious or other values) which a constituency may prize by way of a learning environment for its children.

(iii) Alternative schools usually have smaller enrollments, thereby affording children the extra attention they may require for the development of their learning abilities. A ponderous state system often glosses over the needs of the individual child.

(iv) Smaller systems allow for greater control over such housekeeping matters as teacher selection, student admission and curriculum evaluation.

(v) Special school emphases such as academic excellence are easier to ensure in smaller schools since the constituency for student selection is more limited.

(vi) Since alternative schools usually receive less financial support than public institutions do, additional money input will be required from supporters. This will assure a higher degree of concern and interest on the part of parents and community members, and provide a stronger, more intimate support base for the student.

(vii) Diversity, such as alternative schools provide, reflects and enhances the cultural pluralism of the nation.

Any resolution of the debate about educational diversity on a national scale should be undertaken on sound philosophical bases. An effective starting point for the discussion is to identify the issues and suggest several possibilities for consideration. The greatest difficulty in this regard will be to generate philosophical and pedagogical concerns rather than emotional rhetoric. If philosophic assumptions are not made clear, as John Dewey warned, education may be conducted blindly, under the control of customs and traditions that have never been examined, or in response to immediate social pressures.

The *first* question has a rather obvious answer; should diversity in schooling be encouraged, and the answer must be affirmative. The fact is that alternative kinds of schools do function quite well and they often manage to achieve their goals. The question is, can they only do their job outside of a public system? It is safe to assume that democratic nations like Canada and the United States can withstand a minor degree of variation in schooling in the same way that they foster variation in other basic institutions. Variation encourages creativity and makes choice available. It may also serve as a check and may spur a higher standard of delivery on the part of larger educational systems.

Second, the question as to format, standards and legal requirements must be raised. Should alternative schools have certified teachers, use state-approved curricula and be subject to periodic state-originated inspection? The obvious answer is affirmative based on the assumption that some semblance of national education is to be preserved, but surely minor concessions could be made to those sectors desiring diversity, whether one argues for the freedom to educate on the grounds of Scripture, law or common sense. Alternative institutions should have nothing to hide, so why would it be necessary for them to function primarily as reactionary models in order to be effective? Were these schools not also designed to prepare the young for full participation in citizenship activities?

Third, is the question of funding, and while historically both the United States and Canada have arranged that separate and/or parochial schools can at least receive partial funding from the state, that decision must constantly be open to review as conditions change.

The *fourth* question is perhaps more fundamental and pertains to the matter of whose children are being educated. Do parents own their children? Are children the property of the state? To what extent should these parties cooperate in providing functional education for the young?

Regardless of what kind of approach to diversity is taken, it should be remembered that the democratic way will be assured when single-mindedness is avoided and respect for pluralism and creativity is made a priority. It would not hurt, by the way, to remember that the future of the nations' children is at stake.

Historical Roots

Although the clamor for alternative schools in North America was highlighted in the 1970s, the first such institution was actually begun in Europe by Maria Montessori in 1907. Five years later Anne George opened the first American Montessori school in Tarrytown, New York. Shortly thereafter several independent and private schools following the Montessori model were developed in other locations. The base presupposition of Montessori's thinking was to help young children develop autonomy and self-direction through freedom of movement. Children were free to determine at any time which of several activities they chose to undertake. Essentially the Montessori concept lay dormant until the 1960s when the push for alternative schools revived (Glatthorn, 1975).

A second approach to envisaging alternatives in education before the 1970s was promoted by progressive educators who followed the lead of John

Dewey and Harold Rugg. The Progressive Education Association began in 1919 and motivated the establishment of such schools as the Children's School (later the Walden School), the Dalton School, and the Oak Lane Country School, by placing emphasis on children's emerging interests as the focal point in curriculum-making. Despite the decline of the Progressive Association in the 1950s splinter groups kept the concept alive at the elementary school level. Alternatives at the secondary level, however, were scant. A few schools experimented with progressive ideas but the effect on institutional schooling was minimal.

One example of alternative education was developed in 1919 by Carleton W. Washburne, superintendent of the Winnetka Public School System, a suburb of Chicago. Washburne devised a twofold objective: (i) to analyze course content into specific objectives, and (ii) devise a plan of instruction so that students would be allowed to master each of the objectives at their own rate. Teachers were instructed to break down their courses into specific objectives and students would be expected to scrutinize and comprehend the final list for each course. As students progressed, performance tests were made available at various points so that students could see how well they were doing. Whenever a test was passed with one hundred percent, the student was allowed to proceed to the next phase of the course.

The significance of the Winnetka Plan lay in its attempt to provide for individual differences in learning and, at the same time, teach for specific, clearly identifiable objectives. In one sense the plan was a return to the days of recitation since students were expected to earn a perfect score on a test before they were allowed to proceed further. Analysts Bayles and Hood (1966) have argued that the widespread use of workbooks in American education attests to the pervasive and continuing influence of the Winnetka movement on curriculum and teaching methodology.

In 1925 educator Henry Clinton Morrison developed a "unit plan" to accommodate individualized instruction for American high schools. Essentially his idea necessitated use of new vocabulary more than anything else. Morrison conjectured that if textbook chapters were recast as units, students could be encouraged to master a series of units for a course which would result in their attaining a "special ability" representative of "a personality adaptation" (Bayles and Hood, 1966). When students undertook a particular unit of study, they were expected to fulfil five steps: first, a pretest was undertaken to determine the extent of student familiarity with the unit. *Second,* if the student experienced any difficulty with the content, a diagnosis was undertaken to identify a possible remedy. *Third,* procedures were adapted in order to influence student success. The *fourth* step was again to teach the unit and as a final step retest the student. This procedure was followed until the student had mastered the unit and was then allowed to go on to the next. In each instance the target of the operation was for students to understand the material under consideration but content was not open to review. The selection of subject matter was not open to examination and students were not encouraged to reflect on or conjecture implications of any problems or concepts under scrutiny. Although both the Winnetka Plan and Morrison Plan promised alternative ways of delivering schooling, in a real sense their approaches simply recast old ways in new vocabulary.

Later Developments

A 1971 Gallup poll reported that sixty percent of parents in tne United States whose children were enrolled in public schools were satisfied with the education their children were receiving. The remaining forty percent were ripe targets for those who campaigned on the slogan of choosing a school appropriate to children's needs and learning styles. The difficulty was that alternative schools had no theoretical base and little history to build on. Proponents of these schools knew what they were against, but they had little concept of what they were for. Curricula, evaluation techniques, school design and structure and teacher training programs were all geared to the traditional model, so where should the revolution begin?

Two major concerns of the alternative camp during the 1970s were the alleged failure of public schools to teach basic skills, and the promotion of elitism (Tonsmeire, 1977). Some children were simply receiving a better education than others. To improve on the first deficiency, alternative educators sought to broaden the concept of teaching the 3 R's by methods other than rote and drill. This despite the fact that it had not been established that those were the primary methods employed by public school teachers. Still, a "revolution" has to start somewhere, even if only by building straw men. After alternative schools began to appear on the educational landscape with some degree of regularity, it was the turn of public school supporters to lay claims that alternative schools were ignoring the teaching of basic skills which they had promulgated as a primary objective for the formation of these institutions. Suddenly, they too were much more involved with developing environments in which concern for the "whole child" could be fostered.

As part of the backlash to criticism, proponents of alternative schools charged public schools with fostering elitism since there were glaring forms of inequity evident in the quality of public school programs in some states. Although the elitist charge was essentially without ground, when the dust had settled, there were convincing arguments that the exclusivism of alternative schools matched in intensity any forms of stratification fostered in public schools. It was and still is certainly true that all public schools are not equal, but as shown in the previous chapter, this is more a feature of nonpublic schools than public. Alternative and private schools sometimes have better facilities and offer a broader range of programs than do public schools because their constituents can respond more favorably to fund-raising campaigns.

Alternative schools have tended to draw their enrollments from specific constituencies, thereby portraying themselves as institutions that appeal to groups sporting unique philosophies. Since their numbers are relatively small, however, compared to the number of public schools in any district, these schools often appear as unusual, unique or reactionary as opposed to public schools. When the 1970s were over, the alternative schools movement had peaked, partially because one form of disillusionment with public education was over. Today they seem to have resurfaced formally under the guise of charter schools and informally as home schooling.

The Financial Factor

One of the pressures put on public schooling by critics and alternative seekers has been the complaint that public schools are financially inefficient; they do not deliver on the dollar. Somehow this metaphor always has educators cringing – or being defensive. After all, the notion that schools should be evaluated by productivity in terms of dollars and cents in the same manner that any factory would be has educators worried, and for good reason. Bottles or cans in a canning factory probably all look the same and pretty much are the same; the point is, that it does not matter if they are or are not the same. They are there for one purpose. Anyone trying to tack this metaphor onto the developmental processes of the average child is simply making a category mistake. Students constitute an entirely different species from bottles and cans. Despite this reality and the persistent reactions of educators, the factory metaphor persists. In the 1970s, for example, a cry went up to install competency testing in America's public schools. By the decade's end, over half of the American states had legislated some form of competency-based testing requirements. No one can say that state legislators do not respond to the demands of their constituents. What matters is that theirs be sensible and defensible responses.

Despite this rather uninformed view of how children grow and develop and learn, the quest to build choice into schooling based on financial considerations is neither new nor finished. The movement probably began in sincerity in the form of the voucher system, based largely in the USA, although Canada had its own facsimiles of the concept. In the voucher arrangement, parents are given access to direct money grants which they can trade for the education of their children at the school of their choice. An underlying assumption of this plan is that parents feel more committed to a particular school if they have a greater voice in its selection, and what greater "voice" than money? Proponents of the concept believe that teachers will be more responsive to student needs if they know that dollars for enrollments are on the line in relation to their professional behavior. In addition, the arrangement originally guaranteed that school programs would more nearly reflect the concerns of the constituency about school ongoings. Individual needs of students would also be met to a greater degree as flexibility and a catering to constituent demands would be standard in the arrangement.

The first real published account of a voucher experiment occurred in 1955 when Milton Friedman, an economist, decided that government monopoly in education was a threat to the system itself (Young, 1981). His proposal received widespread acceptance and proponents for the plan sprang up quickly in all sectors of American society.

The Voucher Plan

Friedman's original proposal for a voucher system was a relatively unregulated concept but it was aimed at limiting government involvement in schooling. Friedman suggested that individual schools should be allowed to set their own admission standards as long as they did not offend the freedom of any American child. These schools should not be allowed to discriminate in student selection, although tuition costs for participants in any given school could vary. School officials should be able to make extra charges to any parents who wanted a "better" education for their children, but the bottom line of assurance was that schools would admit any students from within the nation and guarantee them a basic, workable education. Equal access to basic education was the fundamental plank of this plan, but it is easy to see how it could be abused by those who had access to greater sources of funding. Wealthier parents were simply able to offer their children a fuller, more complete education with all the "extras."

By the mid-1960s, when the theme of alternative schooling was in vogue the voucher plan was given serious attention in some sectors, particularly by those who felt that a more competitive spirit would arouse American education from its lethargy. Theodore Sizer, Dean of the Harvard Graduate School, suggested that in all fairness vouchers should be awarded only to families of lower socio-economic status. He also suggested that government subsidies to these families could gradually be reduced in proportion to family income. Another Harvard academic, Christopher Jencks, argued for careful government regulation of the voucher system and claimed that no parents should be allowed to supplement vouchers with private resources. Jencks also suggested that children from poor families should receive a special compensatory voucher which could be used to help school graduates to appear more acceptable in a free market society. This arrangement was viewed by Jencks as an opportunity to make resources available to schools for solving some of the problems often associated with poverty.

As the decade unfolded the new market spawned a variety of related proposals, of which the following characteristics were typical: (i) schools could charge what they wanted for tuition as long as they provided scholarships for the poor; (ii) the amount charged for tuition could not be more than the voucher amount and financial assistance could be lobbied for by each school; and, (iii) schools would be rewarded for student achievement by government sources, and penalized for failure to bring about a certain level of achievement for all students. Achievement levels would be determined by standardized tests. At first glance the proposed arrangement immediately led observers to the conclusion that a myriad of hidden agendas were implicit in the plan. Some originators clearly had their eyes fixed on the relative market values of education and therefore encouraged all kinds of competition, while others agitated for a more regulated system that would expand freedom of choice. The latter often saw the need for enhancing diversity as a means of maximizing individual needs and enriching the nation's multicultural climate.

More specifically, it was Friedman's unregulated market model which promoted the concept that every household in America would be issued a voucher with the same redeemable value for each child in the nation at a school of the parent's choice. All schools could charge tuition to the amount of the voucher which would initially be legislated at a level equal to the existing cost of educating a child in any given district. Another voucher plan, the Sizer-Whitten model, was known as the unregulated compensatory model and boosted the value of vouchers for children from poorer families. Essentially, schools could charge whatever amount of tuition they felt appropriate, but families with incomes above a certain level, would receive no compensation. At a given point, the value of the vouchers would be zero.

Christopher Jencks devised a private membership model which posed that schools could charge any amount of tuition they wanted, provided they gave scholarships to children from lower income families. Jencks proposed the establishment of a central voucher agency that would design a formula by which to show how much people at each income level would be charged. Another model, known as the Coon-Sugarman voucher model, followed up on this idea and formulated the establishment of several different levels per student expenditure, and allowed schools to set their own levels. Parents who chose higher levels of tuition-type schools could do the same and draw on the extra cash available to them. Poorer families could do the same and draw on their voucher potential to cover the cost of tuition.

Then, as if there were not enough models to choose from, two additional proposals cropped up in the form of the egalitarian model and the achievement model which fostered related but slightly different approaches. The egalitarian model posed that the value of vouchers would be the same for every child, and no school should be allowed to charge extra tuition. Instead, schools should be able to solicit funds for special programs from government and private sources or encourage fund-raising via community or support organizations. The achievement approach advocated that the value of vouchers would be based on progress made by students during the school year. Schools would be rewarded if their students exceeded predicted scholastic levels or penalized if the reverse occurred. Schools could contract achievement levels where monies were proportioned to gains on standardized tests.

Few of the proposed models, with the exception of Jenck's private membership model and Coons-Sugarman approach, were ever tested in action. The unofficial title for Jenck's model was the Alum Rock Experiment. The Coons-Sugarman approach was also known as the California Family Choice Program. A brief description of each program will illustrate the complexities of trying to improve public education by "refining" equal opportunity.

The Alum Rock Experiment

The Center for the Study of Public Policy at Cambridge, Massachusetts, initially set about testing Jencks' voucher system by establishing several demonstration programs in heterogeneous communities. Primarily concerned with assisting underprivileged children, advocates recommended that initial grants be given to selected communities and demonstrations themselves were to last from five to eight years. In September, 1972, the Community of Alum Rock, California, decided to implement the plan on a larger scale, the only one of several American communities to really do so. Because of its appreciation for innovation, the community was allowed to make significant changes to the basic model, first of all by involving only six of its sixteen schools, all of them public.

The Alum Rock experiment began by developing a control centre known as the Educational Voucher Agency which would ensure a school's eligibility by requiring the use of a certain curriculum in order to assure the avoidance of discrimination in its operation. Every aspect of the participating school's program was investigated, including transportation and staffing. Specifically, the following policies were adopted: (i) no school would charge tuition beyond that allowed by the stipulated amount of the voucher; (ii) compensatory vouchers would be given to families of poor children to provide them with incentives to attend school; (iii) if a school had more applicants than space, they would be selected by random means; and, (iv) schools were responsible for providing information to parents.

The results of the Alum Rock experiment were intriguing, to say the least. Influenced to a large extent by the nature of the project rules and the school population itself, participants included students from several specific ethnocultural groups. Fifty-five percent of the original student body had Hispanic backgrounds, ten percent were African Americans, and thirty-five percent had different, yet distinct enthocultural backgrounds. Choice was given to parents in so far as enrollment was concerned, and the autonomy of the school with regard to operation was assured. A questionnaire involving six hundred participants was the basic tool utilized to determine the success of the experiment, and a control group was established for comparisons. It was soon discovered that teachers found the procedure workable and professionally enriching. Enrollments stabilized after the first two years and the project's teachers found themselves able to cope with the business of educating without much further adjustment. Essentially, results of the research were inconclusive, although it was found that amount of education influenced the way parents perceived the project. Those with less formal education were less likely to pay attention to printed materials made available by the experiment's promoters, and, unlike their better educated peers, they also made choices for their children for other than educational reasons.

Teacher enthusiasm for the voucher system emanated from the fact that they felt they had greater control over curriculum, budget and staffing allocations, although this varied from one school to another. Teachers frequently identified very strongly with their particular school and were reluctant to transfer if the need arose. Although only a half dozen schools were involved in the study, these were further subdivided into twenty-two "mini schools." Specifically, teachers cooperated to the extent that conditions in their mini-systems were not threatened. One complaint was that the competitive nature of the experiment added to the amount of problems teachers faced in the regular system instead of solving them. Thus the dilemma arose that if problems were even partially seen to be resolved, the enrollment of the school would increase and problems would be enhanced.

Enrollment figures in the Alum Rock project schools fluctuated. After an initial increase of up to sixty percent enrollment in one mini-school, a ten percent figure of change appeared to normalize. As choices became standardized, variations in enrollment between years two and three became more moderate. In so far as choice was concerned, parents appeared to take advantage of their options to a marked degree in the initial stages of the plan and later either wearied of the process, saw no real differences in approaches, or simply became concerned with other matters.

Critics of the Alum Rock experiment ranged widely in their perspectives, some claiming that the operators did not go far enough in their quest to encourage choice or, for that matter, to make genuine options available. Apparently, some schools took action to reduce their vulnerability by building cash revenues and placing limits on acceptance of students and enrollments. The fact that only public schools were included was another concern of critics, thus limiting testing to a specified group with alleged advantages that were intriguing to say the least. These included smaller classes, more attention to the needs of the slow learners and higher achievers, parental choice in schooling, and the inclusion of multi-age groups in the student body. To some extent these features would be expected in an experimental setting since the control of debilitating factors would be maximized in order to make the program look as successful as possible.

Critics of the Alum Rock Program cautioned that if the experiment were expanded, it would eventually destroy public education. Freeman Butts (1979) objected to any manipulation of public education funding and warned against the dangers of the experiment on historical grounds. He argued that Thomas Jefferson's idea of democratic education would be dismantled by a voucher system by creating hidden inequalities and by feeding the thirst for privatism. For Butts, and those who sided with him, it was all or nothing. Why be hasty in significantly altering a system that had successfully produced national leaders, inventors, and scientists, to say nothing of millions of satisfied "clients"?

The California Family Choice Initiative

The California Family Choice Initiative was the brain child of John Coons (1979) and Stephen Sugarman (1980) of the University of California at Berkeley, who conceived the idea of a series of independent schools that would be created by a vote of existing school boards. The inception of such a plan was arranged to occur by a petition with enough signatures from interested parents within a particular school district. Incentives for developing independent schools would be fostered by a deregulation of existing rules to provide additional flexibility so that the schools could be developed by either parental groups or other interest groups. Every school could establish its own kind of administration patterns but administrators would not be permitted to enroll more than their allowable numbers. If the school had more applicants than could be accommodated, a lottery system would have to be inaugurated. Children could be expelled only for extraordinary reasons.

Standard features of the California Family Choice Initiative program included teacher bargaining, a tax-originated financial base, and arrangements for special student needs. A system of teacher awards was designed for those who filled the office well, part of the basic focus being to guarantee the best education for all. What was unique about the plan was to create real variation in school programs and orientation, but the traditional notion of operating schools via a publicly elected board of trustees remained. Although the system was never inaugurated because of the failure to garner a sufficient number of votes, proponents were anxious to gear up for a second try at a later date (Santo, 1980).

By 1995 at least fourteen state legislatures had passed laws permitting exploration in "school choices" as an answer to what were perceived as the "ills" of public schooling. The 1992 and 1996 presidential elections reflected public interest in forms of the voucher plan although educators were generally opposed to them. The strongest propulsion to promoting vouchers was premised on the assumption that they would encourage competition and students' academic capabilities would be increased. Recent research on vouchers in Britain, France and the Netherlands, however, reveals that they have tended to widen the gap between the privileged and underprivileged (Sianjina, 1999). As financial school support declined in the 1980s, parents with higher incomes saw to it that the schools their children were attending were supported, while parents with lower incomes were unable to do so. Another objection to vouchers has arisen from the fact that many schools that benefitted from a voucher plan have been private, religiously-sponsored schools, a fact that violates the highly valued American concept of separation of church and state.

Any school arrangement that undermines public education, directly or inadvertently promotes social stratification, and allows rampant elitism to foster in training the young, must certainly be put under sharp scrutiny. If it contributes to unfairness by abolishing equal opportunity, it must certainly be abolished or amended. If inequity is permitted to prevail, it is of great concern that some young people will end up being rejected by an institution that allegedly exists primarily to equip them intellectually and provide them with opportunity, not take it away.

Reviewing Vouchers

It is difficult to formulate an instrument to evaluate the various voucher plans because most of them were never fully put into operation. The concept was probably too radical even for late twentieth century thinking. One of the factors in assessing any of these proposals is the role of government; some plans proposed a limited role for government in terms of distribution of funds only while others foresaw some involvement in terms of delivery as well. A further involvement might pertain to the assurance of non-discriminatory practices or to manage available school space to assure maximum usage among participating schools in a given district.

Philosophically, the voucher concept promulgates many revered ideas among avant garde educators such as economic equality, healthy competition, commitment, shared values and a broader scale for educational advancement (Johnson, 1982). Accountability would be more specifically directed at parents, thereby assuring a more explicit meaning to the notion of democratic rights, and a wider range of schools from which to choose would also relieve pressures on sectarian and private schools.

Claims that a school system highlighted by a voucher plan would be more academically effective or more cost efficient was not borne out by a study of Chile's experience (McEwan and Carnoy, 2000). In 1980, Chile's military government initiated sweeping educational reforms that saw the transfer of public school management shift from the Ministry of Education to local municipalities. Committed to decentralization, the Chilean government altered how public and private schools were financed by disbursing monthly payments to municipalities based on a fixed voucher multiplied by the number of students enrolled in their schools. Soon many schools that were formerly private entered the voucher system so that by 1996, 81 of Chile's 334 municipalities did not have a single privately-run school.

McEwan and Carnoy's study (2000) of the various school types that resulted from this arrangement in Chile revealed that Catholic-run voucher schools were somewhat more costly than those run by municipalities, while non-religious voucher schools (some of them organized on a for-profit basis) were less costly. The latter were even marginally less effective than public schools in producing higher achievements in Spanish and mathematics. These schools were even less effective when located outside the capital city of Santiago. This indicates that in Chile's voucher system the new players were non-religious, for-profit schools. They successfully competed with public schools by cutting costs but did not raise expected academic achievement. In fact, some of their cost reduction strategies may have contributed to lower academic achievement.

Some educators have protested that schools are not particularly appropriate institutions to be charged with the mandate of equalizing opportunity, and the voucher plan therefore has the potential to create a system of "private" schools supported by public funds. The claim to avoid discriminatory practices is still another concern of voucher critics who suggest that elitism could result from the use of such criteria as income, academic ability or religion if utilized as a basis for admission. The exact nature of the process can hardly be guaranteed and this makes it highly susceptible to personal ingenuities in giving the appearance of equality. Finally, the exclusion of religious schools from the voucher system, some argue, would leave the public system virtually unchallenged anyway.

Philosophically, the question needs to be raised as to the feasibility of converting a "soft-ware" enterprise like schooling into a business model. What kind of educational reforms can be expected from subjecting schooling to a model based on profit and loss statements? Are the concerns of the two systems similar in all respects? What are the assurances that both the initial concept and continual monitoring of the process will have essential peda-

gogical input from professional educators? If the system is run by traditional functionaries and based on established notions of what schooling can or
should do, will the result really be any different?

Frequently, private schools are held up to be an example of the potential
success of a voucher system with the corollary argument that these schools
"play to an open market" and fare quite well at it. What is different, however, is the fact that private schools cater to a select market (usually from within the religious community), and what they offer is not to be envisaged to be
in the same category as the basic education offered by the public system.
Private schools usually have to charge tuition rates that are not affordable by
lower income families (unless by very dedicated people), and they feature a
reduced student-teacher ratio. Some of these schools also utilize an entrance
test that assures them of a select student body; apparently, voucher schools
would not be allowed to do this.

It has often been suggested that the initiation of a voucher plan would
provide more choices for parents in selecting schools for their children. An
analysis of this claim by (Whitty, et al., 1998) indicate that an open-ended
voucher scheme would clearly benefit households that are more affluent than
average, although some might believe that making vouchers available to
everyone would open up private schools to the poor. Whitty and associates
disagree, charging that the opposite effect might be equally plausible. With
more money available, private schools that cannot currently afford to select,
such as some inner-city private schools, could become more selective. These
already highly selective schools could then maintain their advantage by
demanding add-on payments in addition to vouchers.

The economic base on which the voucher debate has raged fosters a bit
of redeemable philosophical ground, but little of it has been directed towards
the improvement of the teaching situation or the rights of the teaching profession. Coons (1979) pled for an equitable system of schooling that would
once and for all eliminate class segregation in schooling, and Sugarman
(1980) stressed the need to restore choice into the enterprise. He suggested
that there seemed to be consensus over what the proper goals and means of
education ought to be, so why not let people choose what form of schooling
they desired for their children (within certain limits, of course). John
Goodman expressed sympathy for the voucher concept, but complained
about the lack of attention afforded "essential knowledge and universal
truths" in contemporary schools.

The emergence of charter schools, which allegedly represent public
interests to a greater extent than private schools, has motivated some critics
to observe that these schools would be more justified recipients of voucher
monies than private schools. Instead of public dollars going to private
schools, the money could be directed towards schools that are more public in

philosophy and representation. This proposal will be discussed in more detail in a later chapter.

Tuition Tax Credits

In 1983 the US Supreme Court upheld the decision of the Minnesota State Department of Education to allow a tax deduction for educational expenses pertaining to parental school choices. This privilege permitted parents of both public and private school children to deduct educational expenses of up to $650 per elementary school child and $1 000 per secondary school student from their income when calculating their annual income tax. Basically the privilege did not really offer financial advantages to parents of public school students since parents do not normally pay much to have their children attend public schools. Thus this subsidy largely benefitted parents who chose to send their children to private schools (Darling et al., 1988).

The Minnesota case had its origins in an announcement made by American President Ronald Reagan on April 15, 1982, when he addressed the annual meeting of the National Catholic Educational Association. Reagan announced that he would install a means whereby parents who opted for private schooling for their children would be able to deduct a portion of the tuition expenses from their income tax. Reagan's rationale for making this proposal included the observation that America should be perceived as the greatest and freest nation in the world. Yet, in a free land, people were not being given the right to choose the form of education they wished for their children. Reagan professed to change that, at least to some extent, but his government restricted parents from applying the scheme to the college level because of financial restraints. Reagan reiterated many themes common to US education in his address, including reference to the Pledge of Allegiance, but insisting that he was on the side of improving education, not tearing it down by encouraging alternatives. He suggested that since knowledge is intricately connected to freedom, alternatives in American education would only serve the best interests of the cause of different avenues if the pursuit of knowledge were encouraged. He also implied that the nation's poor would benefit from the plan because they would now be able to afford to educate their children in some of the nation's finest schools if they chose to do so.

In actuality the ground for Reagan's tuition tax credit plan was based in the 1960s when private school enrollments began to decline. Supporters rallied to beseech the government for some form of financial assistance, arguing that private schools were an important alternative to public education. Their only success was to maintain tax exempt status for these schools. In the 1970s private school enrollments again climbed, partially as a result of mandatory desegregation, and parents again complained to the government about the high costs of private education. Under the Carter Administration, what was called the Packwood-Moynihan Tuition Tax Credit Bill, was prepared to allow private school supporters to deduct a maximum of 50 percent of their tuition costs from their income tax up to a maximum of $500. The bill was defeated on the basis that it would cost too much in lost tax revenue, but it took the convincing of the Reagan Administration to bring the essence of the Packman-Moynihan proposal into effect. Undoubtedly the passing of the bill was influenced by the publication of the Coleman Report which was seen as encouraging of private schools. In 1983 Reagan initially proposed a one hundred dollar limit on tax credits which was raised to higher amounts later on.

Debating Tuition Tax Credits

Central to any debate on education in America is the Constitutional matter of the separation of church and state. The bulk of literature on the subject favors the proposal to allow tax credits, and most defenders justify their stand constitutionally on the basis that these credits may only be used by individuals, not by institutions. This stance apparently circumvents the possibility of constitutional violations, but it still does not stifle the voices of those who favor public education at all costs. These critics claim that if private or parochial education is assisted in this manner, it will ultimately undermine public education. If the ground for ensuing this path is the assumption that public education has failed in some way, additional money should be awarded that institution so it may be improved in the areas in which it has been deficient.

Proponents of tuition tax credits argue that private schools have a legal and democratic right to exist because of the justice implied in the American pluralist principle, and maintain that families with lower incomes would benefit most from such a scheme. It is true that parents who opt to send their children to private schools not only bear the cost of their children's private education but they also pay taxes to support the public school as well. That, public school proponents contend, can hardly be considered a violation of American fair play. After all, the nation provides public schooling to all citizens. Extras should cost money.

A rigorous analysis of tuition tax credits was undertaken by David W. Breneman. Breneman (1983) argued that since public schools do not charge tuition, a tuition tax credit for elementary-secondary schooling markedly changes the relative costs to parents of both public and private schools by reducing the price differential by the amount of the credit. As a result, one should expect some parents to transfer their children to private schools, thereby working a hardship on public schools. Of course, much of the interest and debate focusses on the size and socio-economic composition of the group most likely to make the shift. Breneman was also concerned that the allowance of tuition tax credits could legitimize private schools that really do not deserve such status.

Perhaps the most common complaint about tuition tax credits is that they foster the demise of the public school system. Hawkins (1982) argues that the public system is presently overburdened with assignments, having to be "all things to all people," and is thus unable to deliver on all counts. Besides having to provide students with a sound education, schools have become active in guaranteeing human rights and assuring services to the disabled. These are certainly laudable goals, but many of them are simply beyond the capability of the institution because they require a specialization which is impossible for a generalist institution to deliver. Combined with this schools have also had to contend with cry for the return to "the basics" (Hawkins, 1982: 9).

It has been argued that the case for tuition tax credits contributes to the availability of choice in education (Baldwin, 1982). Premised on the notion that diversity can foster better and cheaper schools by bringing a little healthy competition to the scenario, it is claimed that such an arrangement will better reflect the diversity inherent in the nation's makeup. If societal differences can be accommodated in an institution as significant as the school, it will provide a higher degree of happiness to the citizenry and contribute to the quality of life. Pushed a little further, however, it may also be pointed out that too much competition may also diminish the fundamental objective of schooling, namely to educate students, and substitute a market value aura to the school instead. In addition, diversity in excess can easily lead to duplication or splintering or even reduction in quality. Another frequently cited argument favoring tuition tax credits is the savings to be enjoyed by people with lower incomes. The truth of the matter is that the actual amounts saved by the average family is minuscule when the reality of a comparatively small tax deduction is calculated.

Essentially the groundswell in favor of tuition tax credits rests on the same philosophical laurels as proposals for vouchers. The central alleged purpose of both schemes is to meet social needs, and the most frequently touted advantage is to assist lower income groups and provide a more equitable system of education. Related advantages apparently include reduction of financial pressures on private schools through increased parental commitment and enthusiasm. Research on private education has shown this not to be the case but that fact has been embellished to suggest that smaller targets of commitment, which private schools represent, are objects of intensified dedication.

Performance Contracting

The decade of the 1970s witnessed a continual barrage of complaints against public schools. A familiar cry was for greater accountability of schools to ensure productivity. Dissatisfied with the performance of schooling generally, a trend soon began to award some of the school's functions to private industries which promised greater guarantees than educators in the public education system. Although the demand for greater accountability was often articulated by politicians, Zentner (1972) suggested that it had its most immediate support among those less-educated taxpayers whose children experienced success neither in the school system nor in the marketplace.

Essentially, performance contracting is an agreement made between an educational authority and a private corporation in which the latter agrees to supervise and/or conduct particularized learning activities which will result in specified levels of attainment as assured by mutually agreed upon criteria. In the arrangement, the educational authority will pay the corporation fixed amounts for certain performance levels per student within specified times (McConville, 1973).

The rationale for electing to initiate performance contracting was derived from several assumptions, one of them being the notion that the education system is supported by the community and should be accountable to the community. By contracting educational activities to private sources that represent the community, accountability would be much more evident than what the school could deliver since industry would be trying harder to accomplish announced goals.

Another impetuous for the plan had to do with the complaint that schools were too oriented towards average students and low achievers were often neglected. By assigning teaching tasks specifically related to individual student needs, pressure to perform would increase on the part of private entrepreneurs and learning would thus be enhanced. (Mecklenburger, 1972). Proponents of performance contracting also argued that a different environment than "normal" was necessary to motivate slower learners to achieve; they contended that higher achievers learned through pressure from their peers, but slow learners were not so motivated. Therefore, if slow learners were taken from the public school environment and placed in another, more competitive environment, they might develop added motivation to learn.

The envisaged non-school environment was to be designed to focus on possible material rewards, a concept not typical of school environments but apparently pedagogically feasible (Reed, 1972). Experiments of an extraordinary nature were never allowed in public schools, it was argued, part of the problem being that administrators were usually too busy to pay much attention to new possibilities or procedures. Consequently, slow learners and other groups of students were often neglected because of the rush to get on with assigned programs. As outsiders, free from the constraints of regular schooling, performance contractors could devise their own environments in which even radical teaching methodologies could be practiced. There were some educators who fought against the notion of incentives on the basis that the plan could become part of the socialization process and thus confuse students into believing that life basically functions according to the attainment of rewards.

The original assignment of performance contracts was based on the premise that only bona fide educators would be employed by contracted firms in order to assure a professionally competent delivery. No contract was to be negotiated that would undermine the integrity of the public school or its responsibilities to children. Care was also supposed to be taken to avoid signing contracts just because they had been made to look attractive by clever sales gimmicks. Also, the motivation of the potential firm to be employed was checked out to ensure that the program would not simply deteriorate into a propaganda campaign or the pursuit of the self-interests of the company. Another caveat was to appraise the company's contract with regard to the inclusion of professional attitudes, ideas and motivations since the field was full of prospective agents almost as soon as the movement got underway. The assumption on which many proponents from within the educational world proceeded was that most industries were probably honest and upright but extra precautions needed to be taken because the nation's children were the primary targets of the plan. That fact came to light again and again as controversy raged about the movement over the next decade.

The performance contracting movement rested heavily on the notion of accountability, which suggested that playing to that piper would also augur well for the teaching profession. Lassinger (1971) identified a series of ways in which this might happen. In the first instance, the focus of teaching could shift to more informal methods and teachers would be able to utilize a much wider range of non-school resources. Student achievement would become a major objective of the program, salary levels would be increased, and teacher training institutions would be called upon to emphasize competence in enhancing student learning as a major criterion for admitting trainees. These were indeed valued hopes.

The American Federation of Teachers opposed performance contracting on the basis that its inauguration would take educational policy-making out of the hands of the public and give it to private industrial entrepreneurs. Performance contracting would allow the development of a business-run monopoly and dehumanize the teaching-learning process. With achievement as an esteemed goal, teachers would be called upon to teach to standardized tests and teachers would also experience a complete subversion of the bargaining process (Dickinson, 1971).

Critics of performance contracting were not hard to find, for they emerged from nearly all social sectors. The platform on which they found consensus was that schools are not businesses and they were not designed to market services or manufacture products. Schools deal with human beings amidst an array of complicated objectives and any successes must be measured by an entirely unique set of processes. Business is managed by directors and managers whereas schools are run by a governing board selected by the public. Business is an employer, while school is both an employer and a government entity. In the business world power and influence remain within the parameters of the institution itself, while there are many external constituencies operant on decision-making in that context.

The Performance Contracting Plan

Despite its many criticisms, performance contracting was initiated in the United States on a limited basis during the 1970-71 school year. The experiment was managed by the US Office of Economic Opportunity at a cost of 7.2 million dollars. The experiment was concluded in February, 1972; it involved eighteen urban and rural school systems and six contractors, and delivered mixed results. In one contract in Grand Rapids, Michigan, the school board paid a private contractor $75.00 for each student who gained one year of reading achievement, $112.50 for any student who gained one and one-half years of reading achievement, and $127.50 for any student who gained two full years of reading achievement. The contracting company invented what were called "interim performance objectives" worth $37.50 each and payable at intervals during the course of the contract. This kind of arrangement was one of eighteen such contracts negotiated with the US Office of Economic Opportunity (Mecklenburger, 1972).

Proponents of performance contracting argued that the approach was based on sound pedagogical principles and would provide a low risk and cost effective means of experimentation. It would foster racial integration, increase instructional efficiency and humanize the classroom for both students and teachers. Charles Blaschke (1971), a strong proponent of the concept, argued that the plan would encourage better relationships between teachers and students since teachers would smile more at their students since they were being be paid to do so. After a while, Blaschke argued, the put-on smiles might even become real.

Although mathematics and reading were the primary targets of performance contracting, there were also schools where performance in any or all subjects was contracted. For example, in 1970 the Reading Foundation of Chicago contracted with a school in the Compton School District to enroll all seventh graders in a speed reading course for nine weeks. While the company made claims about its successes, educational critics disputed them and were generally in an uproar. They claimed that the company had used inappropriate measuring devices when testing speed and comprehension. The number of words read by students in a given time period were multiplied by the percentage of comprehension obtained. Thus a student could "read" at a very fast rate, obtain a low comprehension score and still appear to have made progress in reading speed. Many students soon discovered that the answers to their comprehension tests were only one page removed from the test itself, and this may have influenced test results (Dembo and Wilson, 1973).

An interesting experiment in performance contracting was launched in Texarcana in 1970 involving eighteen school districts. The site was chosen partially because of the rich ethnic mix of the area and because students were quite far behind in national levels in academic achievement. Altogether 27 000 students were involved in the experiment, of whom 10 800 were taught by private entrepreneurs, 11 880 were in the control group, 1 000 were in special programs and 1 080 were involved in a contract between two school districts and their teachers' groups. The final group of 2 240 were taught in modified programs. The magnitude of the study was sufficiently significant that it virtually became a model for further contracts in the United States.

As the Texarcana experiment got underway, as expected, a serious complaint arose with regard to testing and evaluation. Some doubted that proper testing of skill attainment could really be accomplished, while others warned that if results indeed were positive, there was no assurance that these would be maintained for any significant length of time. In the early stages of contract-making, school trustees discovered that relevant clauses should have been included in contracts made with private companies. The clauses should have had specified penalties to companies if alleged skill gains by students disappeared after six months. By the second year of operation it became evident that there were serious flaws in the plan. Chiefly targeted were such items as the use of inappropriate measuring devices, failure to obtain the services of reliable support groups, that is, people who could handle such items as requests for additional monies, draw up appropriate proposals and monitor the program and convince stakeholders that the program was both viable and legitimate. One school board official who was sold on performance contracting selected several hopeful converts on the board and assigned them to the study of positive contracts on which they could report to the board. Apparently, the tactic worked (*Nation's Schools,* 1971: 33).

The heaviest clouds over Texarcana's sky appeared in conjunction with charges against involved companies for "teaching to the test" and neglecting students' needs. One executive admitted to his company's failure and blamed an overzealous programmer for cramming too much work into too short a period of time. Texarcana School Superintendent, Edward D. Trice, apparently countered criticism by suggesting that any teaching to a test was not good pedagogy (*Nation's Schools,* 1970).

Analysis

Two major defects of performance contracting stand out; the *first* of these is the pervasive myth that turning anything over to the world of business is always a good option. Although the failure of this practice has been documented many times in educational contexts, somehow the belief still lingers (Tanner, 1973). The *second* problematic concern is the notion that ideas for improving schooling can most likely emanate from pretty well any sector other than education. It seems ironic that a society that pays such easy heed to professionals in virtually every other field appears to think that when it comes to the education of their offspring, almost any elected official or business-minded individual is apparently better qualified to improve schooling than professional educators are.

By 1973 the American educational world was ready to admit that performance contracting was under severe scrutiny, mainly because of the difficulty promoters had in defining objectives and achievements other than those involving simple physical skills. The problem arose, of course, because of the human enterprise which is so centrally connected to imperfections, emotion and inexact enactments. Its intricacies are so complex that even the best trained educators will readily admit that a professional team approach is required to properly execute its requirements. Even when therapists, teachers, social workers, counsellors and administrators work together evaluative gaps may emerge. It would be safe to venture a guess that if an experiment was tried which would test the hypothesis that educators make the best educators, it might not only be a first in North American history, it might also constitute a first instance in education of putting the horse before the cart.

Promoters of performance contracting have frequently voiced their disdain with teachers and educational administrators for not supporting their cause, but the truth is that the arrangement simply wrests authority from one nonprofessional agency (trustees) and assigns it to another (private business). In the meantime, educators have rarely been consulted about this transfer of power. As it is, teachers are frequently viewed as dispensable to the process of education, and too much the view is perpetuated that almost anyone can teach, regardless of qualifications. This view justifies such phenomena as home schooling and the establishment of non-registered private schools run by organizations with hidden agendas. To a certain extent teachers themselves have been to blame because they have taken this form of professional abuse without getting very agitated about it. When it came to stopping performance contracting, however, their influence has been justified and immense.

But performance contracting is not dead. In 1992 nine public schools in Baltimore contracted out the education of their students to a private organization known as Education Alternatives Incorporated (EAI). EAI authorities claimed they could educate students for less money than public schools and even turn a profit. After only one year EAI officials had to admit that their students were not doing any better than their counterparts in public schools and, moreover, the plan had not proven to be particularly profitable for EAI. Despite these results Baltimore mayor, Kurt Schmoke, continued the contract with EAI but drew it to a halt after the fourth year. By the fall of 1995 it could be concluded that there were no educational nor financial reasons why the Baltimore school system should continue to contract with EAI. There was no indication at all that students educated by EAI had higher grades or better attendance. As a result of this publicity, EAI stock fell to only five dollars from thirteen dollars a share. Despite this, the following year saw a contract written with Sylvan Learning Systems to tutor children at 29 locations in Baltimore (Pincus, 1996).

The Continued Push

A variety of factors contributed to the campaign to denigrate public education in the mid-twentieth century. If the 1950s could be portrayed as a period of national relief following the Second World War, the 1960s certainly gave indication that the honeymoon was over. A new restlessness originated, partially motivated by the thought of yet another war – this time a questionable war – in Vietnam. As the decade unfolded protests to the war surged, parallelled by the hippie movement which denigrated every aspect of "the establishment." Black power emerged as part of the quest for equal civil rights accompanied by the move to integrate public schools in America. Against this foreground of unrest it was only a small step to questioning the public school agenda. Scrutiny of public schools during the 1970s resulted in the assignment of a business model to education which has not yet been completely eradicated. Those concerned with the improvement of public education continue to ward off this influence, and emphasize the necessity to keep the schools human.

Some plans to improve schools have both pedagogical and humanizing value. For example, a recent restructuring of school scheduling has produced what has been called the year-round school. The rationale for developing this arrangement apparently includes greater use of school facilities and more flexible time on and time-off schedules for both teachers and students. Proponents of the idea also envisage that the new format may contribute towards vision-building, initiative-taking and empowerments, evolutionary planning, monitoring, staff development, and restructuring as key components. For example, in a desire to improve educational opportunities of students, a school community could choose to change to a single-track, year-round calendar in which teachers and students could begin school earlier in the fall and the lost vacation time could be redistributed throughout the school year (Shields and LaRocque, 1998).

Although much of the literature on year-round schooling suggests that a calendar change is associated with increased learning opportunities, there are a number of other factors that have contributed towards a higher success rate in achievement levels. Once school staff become enamored of the idea to make dramatic changes in one segment of school life, this seems to serve as incentive to make other changes as well. For example, year-round schools have been known to make curriculum changes, abolish reliance on textbook-style teaching and revitalize pedagogical procedures. It could be that these changes have also contributed to increased achievement levels for students, but then they may also be indicative of the old adage that any change is better than no change at all. The very suggestion of alteration may be sufficient cause for enhanced motivation for students. In any event, year-round schools are still basically public schools, and despite their rearrangements with the school calendar, they do not threaten the mission or existence of public schools. As Edmonton's public school system has shown, these kinds of alternatives can not only be developed within a given public system, their development within the system assures that any benefits derived therefrom can have widespread benefits.

Six
Home Schooling as Antithesis

North Americans are increasingly becoming aware that it is not required by law for them to send their children to school. In Canada, the law in all ten provinces clearly stipulates that if children are receiving satisfactory instruction in other circumstances, mandatory attendance at public institutions is not required. Provinces vary in the degree to which inspections are made regarding alternative arrangements, but, generally speaking, the system is adequate and fair. People who are aware of their freedom in this regard provide for the education of about 30 000 children in their respective homes in Canada (Patrick, 1998). The Province of Alberta leads the way with over 8 000 children involved in home schooling.

During the 1996-1997 school year 700 000 to 1 150 000 children in grades K-12 were being home schooled in the United States (Taylor, 1997). By 2000 this number was estimated at 1.2 million to 1.7 million home schooled children (McDowell and Ray, 2000). The Home School Legal Defense Association reports that in the United States today every state in the union recognizes home education as legal. The association reports that home schoolers in the United States are presently increasing at a rate of 15 to 20 percent annually. Those who opt for home schooling do so primarily for two reasons; parents remove their children from what they perceive to be negative influences of modernism represented in public schools, and second, because they fear that a secularized version of family life is being promoted in public schools (Butler, 1995).

Why Home Schooling?

According to Van Galen (1991) the rationale for choosing home schooling offered by parents basically breaks down into two camps: those who home educate for religious reasons and those who claim they want to have their children experience innovative pedagogical approaches. Van Galen (1991 labelled the two philosophically different groups of home schooling advocates ideologues and pedagogues. Those in the former camp primarily emphasize the importance of educating their children in line with their fundamental religious beliefs while pedagogues are more concerned about having their children involved in more innovative approaches to learning. Resetar (1990) discovered that parents who were originally motivated by ideological reasons later evaluated their motives and adjusted their thinking to more conventional pedagogical lines.

As home schooling has developed, new forms for doing so have emerged. There are now a considerable number of home schooling families who choose to utilize some aspects of a local public school program in a practice that has come to be known as blended home schooling. Their children attend a local school for part of their education and spend the rest of their time learning at home with a parent. More conservatively religious home schooling parents, however, feel strongly that their children might be damaged by teachings promoted in public schools and they refrain from having anything to do with public schools (Griffith, 1997). Another line of reasoning has been voiced by parents who claim they chose home schooling so that they could be assured their children would avoid possible school violence, poor quality academic school programs and overzealous peer pressure (Schnaiberg, 1996).

The Data Bank of Home Schooling

The data base of information about families who choose to home school reveals that these families are typically white, Protestant, two-parent families with an income that is a little less than the median for all married couples in the United States, but with higher than average educational attainment. Breadwinners in home schooling families appear to represent a variety of occupations (Lines, 1991). The mean size of home schooling families is 3.5 children. Religious preferences of home schooling families in Canada were studied by Ray (1994) and showed that among fathers, 21.1 percent listed their religious preference as independent, fundamental or evangelical in persuasion, 17.9 percent cited "other" or nonreligious, and the rest selected from a provided list of church denominations. Mothers surveyed reported a similar breakdown regarding their backgrounds, with 20.8 percent describing themselves as independent, fundamental, or evangelical, and 17.2 percent as "other" or nonreligious. Thus religious affiliation, particularly conservative forms, played a large part in identifying home schooling families.

A study of the procedures followed in a typical two-parent home schooling situation by Ray (1994) revealed that, in Canada, mothers did 87.88 percent of the teaching, fathers did 9.12 percent of the teaching and other individuals accounted for 2.48 percent of the teaching. A very small percentage of parents involved in home schooling had state-approved teacher certification. Ray found that only 12 percent of the mothers and 7.4 percent of the fathers were legally certified to teach. A study by Priesnitz and Priesnitz (1990) found that only 32 percent of home schooling families followed a specific structured educational format. Thirty percent of those polled reported an unstructured format, and 20 percent reported a child-centred approach. Another 18 percent reported a combination of structured and unstructured styles of teaching.

In recent years home schoolers have built a number of support organizations and networks to their cause, most of which are designed to offer or draw attention to appropriate school curricula and notify home schoolers of coming events of interest. Shellenberger (1998) suggests that home schooling networks often fulfil the role of a school community for home schoolers. Sometimes a number of home schooling families band together to teach their children according to the specialties identifiable among parent group members.

Quite expectedly, the trend to home schooling has raised a number of questions having to do with the enforcement of truancy laws, the ability of the family to adjust to the demands of an added function, and the general flexibility of state laws on schooling. Reasons for extracting children from public (or private) schools are complex, chief of which is a disillusionment with the general impersonality of the public system and an alignment with a value scale that challenges the alleged improprieties of those entrenched in the public system (Klicka, 1993).

Home Schooling Claims

One of the primary concerns of those who opt for home schooling is what they claim public schools do to their children. This cause has brought together an interesting variety of viewpoints or, what John Holt calls, "strange bedfellows." It includes fundamentalist Christians (who are the majority), some of whom do not have much schooling themselves; the back-to-the-landers who do not necessarily align themselves with organized religion; college-educated people, who grow their own food, shun meat, and have babies at home; and, a variety of other groups (Holt, 1983; 1964). Home schooling has also been depicted as a return to the sacred art of mothering (Hunter, 1991). Although home schoolers hold that public schooling does not deliver what it promises, they differ widely in the rationale they use for the withdrawal of their children as well as on the objectives they set for their own educational enterprises.

Dobson (1998), a strong supporter of home schooling, outlines five specific lures that draw parents to opt for home schooling. *First,* is the freedom to choose one's own curriculum and teach one's children whatever one deems to be of importance. *Second*, is having time to spend with one's children, bond with them and become acquainted with their hopes and dreams. A *third* strength is a healthy environment in which to be socialized. *Fourth,* is the strength of choice regarding all aspects of the child's education – rules and regulations, extracurricular activities such as field trips, and learning pace. *Fifth* and finally, Dobson believes that parental love as the pervading spirit of home schooling is the most significant of all benefits.

State Requirements

Although home schooling has generally been accepted in all Canadian provinces for some time, the American states have been more reluctant in their endorsement. The provision for home schooling now exists in all states, but there is still the complicated procedure of satisfying school officials with detailed information about the exact nature of arrangements for instructing children at home. Applicants may use either the first or the fourteenth amendment in making their plea and they must fulfil the requirements of a "compelling interest" test. Primarily, the burden is on the home school family to demonstrate that their religious belief against state-run education is both sincere and consistent. It cannot merely be "philosophical." Second, they must prove that their belief is "burdened" or, restricted by compulsory school attendance (Klicka, 1993: 322). The home school family must also ensure that an acceptable format and appropriate content will be used in home schooling, and the consequences for embarking but failing brings fines in some states and a possible jail term. In many instances this means working closely with a local school board, something which home schoolers generally resent. Evidently, the decision to educate at home is one not to be taken lightly in America (Harris and Fields, 1982). Naturally the legal restrictions placed on home schoolers by the state tend to antagonize them, particularly the requirement to work with local school boards. As one home schooler said, "Some people in other areas are starting to cut their ties [with school boards] because they're not getting anything back from the board and they're being demanded of" (Arnott, 1997: 18). Another home schooler echoed this sentiment; "I would prefer to have no connection with the local school board at all" (Arnott, 1997: 20). One wonders if the attitude of resentment is sufficiently widespread and intense enough to affect the attitudes of the children being home schooled.

The Values Claim

Proponents of home schooling frequently argue that their choice for schooling constitutes a genuine going back to traditional times with an endorsement of traditional values. This assertion can be questioned on the basis that the notion of the "traditional family" as such never was; it is simply a concept that has been firmly planted in people's minds in the form in which they imagine it – probably by the media. Coontz (1992: 27) states that the traditional family is merely "an historical amalgam of structures, values and behaviors that never co-existed in the same time and place." The family style of the 1950s is a good case in point. It was a time when television producers began to mass portray images of desirable family styles. After World War II ended, North Americans suddenly found a new world of satisfaction, amusement and inventiveness within the confines of the nuclear family. In a desperate attempt to keep the economy going, manufacturers and businesses devised the concept of conspicuous consumption and instalment buying to generate revenues previously made possible by the war effort. Factories that previously ground out military products had to be retooled to manufacture consumer goods. Many manufactured goods were deliberately targeted at specific family roles and age groups. Surely this is not the family image desired by home school advocates.

A favorite claim of home school advocates is that they can teach proper values to their children. The underlying assumption of this claim is that if individuals are spoon-fed the correct values, they will unconsciously inculcate them as their own. Simon et al. (1972) found that "moralizing parents" ineffectively teach values because they do not let their offspring make choices for themselves. Home schooling parents will argue that by carefully instructing towards and modelling good choices for their children they will somehow discourage them from making bad choices. Apparently this precaution will safeguard young people from making the same mistakes that their parents might have made. Psychologists will insist, however, that young people raised within the milieu of this perspective are not prepared to make responsible choices on their own when the time comes. They will not have learned how to become aware of nor how to weigh alternatives that determine whether a particular act constitutes a bad choice or a good choice. As a result these individuals can often become ripe targets for yielding to pressure from peers who influence them to make bad choices. Raths et al., (1978) point out that adults, whether teachers or parents, cannot dictate what children's values should be, just as adults cannot dictate what their environments and experiences should be. Values are personal phenomena and value development is a lifelong process. Despite parents' "best" efforts in this regard, some children will still develop alternative ways of thinking and behaving.

In a comparison study of the work values of adults who had been home schooled with those who had attended private, public or separate schools in Alberta, several interesting differences came to light between the two groups – home schoolers and those conventionally-schooled (Friesen, 2001). When compared with conventionally-schooled adults, home schoolers scored lower on seventeen of twenty value scales. In fact, when the data among all four groups was compared, it was discovered that those who had attended Roman Catholic schools deemed general values more important than the other groups. Perhaps the study indicates more than anything that once people reach adulthood they have a way of influencing one another in a manner that wipes out or alters many of their earlier socialization influences.

Analysis

One of the difficulties in describing home schooling is because of the dearth of literature available on the practice, with the exception of that produced by those quite biased towards home schooling. Many home schoolers are resistant to being objects of study, and there is also the problem of identifying a stable population. Many home schooled children are intermittently returned to conventional schools making it difficult to regard them as true representatives of the practice. In addition, many parents do not register young children with their local school, at least in Canada, and officials have no way of knowing what the actual figures for home schooled children might be. Neither would it be possible to determine how these unregistered children might be being educated. In 2000, the *Peabody Journal of Education* made an attempt to alleviate the need for sound research on home schooling and so dedicated an entire enlarged edition of the journal to the topic that featuring both pro and con perspectives.

Two-Way Criticisms

Home school supporters sometimes accuse public schools of depriving children of intellectual and cultural stimulation by teaching with a scope and efficiency considerably less than is needed (Beck, 1990). Apparently this deficiency can be overcome through home schooling but it must be stressed that this can happen only if parents are aware of this shortcoming and are equipped and imaginative enough to handle it. It must also be mentioned that public schools are not all the same; neither do all teachers teach in the same manner. In so far as innovation is concerned, as the previous chapters have outlined, public schools have an admirable record of developing new programs such as community schools, mini-schools, global education, effective schools, year-round education, etc.

Public schools have been accused of enormously distorting children's perceptions of social and political reality and of what is ultimately important in life (Beck, 1990). The vagueness of this criticism constitutes its own explanation in that all public schools cannot be tarred with the same brush. Besides, it could be argued that there is no indication that parents who opt for home schooling are any more psychologically adjusted than public school teachers. Having an axe to grind in the first place probably makes parents who home school even more suspect than public school teachers. Parents who suffer from distorted perceptions probably pass them onto their children relatively intact. Children who attend public schools have a much better chance of coming into contact with a much wider range of perspectives on life and therefore have a wider resource base on which to draw in formulating their personal weltanschauung (world-view).

Proponents of public schools have suggested that home schoolers grow up in single-culture environments with very limited socialization opportunities. In a sense they become culturally hermitized and on attaining adulthood, may lack the skills needed to function in a multicultural society (Arons, 1983). At some point in their lives they will need to learn to get along with people representing a wide range of backgrounds, nationalities, religions and philosophies. Guterson (1992) suggests that extreme isolation of home school children may even amount to a form of child abuse. In rebuttal, home schoolers argue that children who attend conventional schools, and who spend most of their time with peers, become so dependent upon them that they can be negatively influenced by their peers. Of course this argument can be reversed; children who are home schooled by close-minded parents may be better off spending time with classmates who have more positive outlooks on life. Not all peers are bad people, even if they happen to attend conventional schools.

It is often contended that children taught at home tend to score as well or better than their peers in public schools on standardized tests when the tests are required or when they choose to take those tests (Ray, 2000). This is especially important in such areas as the language arts, math, social studies and science. Home schoolers are generally more involved in adult relationships and engage in a variety of group and community activities which effectively serve to supplement their academic activities. In fairness, Ray's (1994) study showed that home school students engage in field trips, group sports, music classes, classes outside the home, volunteer work with people, ballet/dance classes and other activities. In followup studies it has been found that home schooled children who choose to opt into either private or public schools generally do well, and some have been accepted by colleges or universities for further study (Sheffer, 1992). Their participation in postsecondary studies occurs at about the same rate as the national average.

An emerging trend among home schoolers has been to work with neighboring home schooling families in providing a wider educational parameter for their children. Families have often grouped together and formed blended programs in the sense that each parent involved provides aspects of the overall program. This arrangement makes possible a wider resource base and is highly reminiscent of the traditional one-room country school. In one sense home schoolers are developing mini school systems not unlike those that existed all across this continent a generation or two ago (Hill, 2000). Patrick (1998) discovered 8 209 home schooling students engaged in this sort of practice in Alberta.

People who endorse home schooling are generally very adamant about it being the best possible approach to teaching and learning. Proudly they claim that home schooling is more cost effective; it develops independent thinkers and leaders, builds character, and even provides a superior foundation for international friendship and understanding (Harris, 1988). Unfortunately, these strong-minded proponents also denigrate public education as the enemy and private schools as a tolerated, but inadequate format. When promulgated from a religious (Christian) perspective, promoters of home schooling like to portray the public system as brazenly secular or humanistic in orientation, and therefore unacceptable. This stance disregards the fact that thousands of Christians enroll their children in both private and public schools by choice, and are convinced that their faith is not under threat in those systems. It is difficult to understand how home schoolers can "graduate" with a better attitude towards "building international understanding and friendship" when trained by leaders who foster such negativism towards traditional forms of schooling. As Lubienski (2000) notes, home schooling, by its very nature, denies the public interest by acknowledging no mechanism and no legitimate public interest in the education of "other people's children." This is most unfortunate because the public school represents the one institution that is most open to public input through traditions of local control, elections, public gatherings and school conferences.

Seven
Charter Schools: New Kid on the Block

Charter schools have appeared on the North American scene like gang-busters. These schools have basically been promoted on the promise of providing a greater range of choices for parents to educate their children. However, this is not the foundation on which the charter school movement began. The concept of charter school first emerged in New Zealand where it was the intent of the originators that the formation of charter schools would encourage additional local interest and reflect local culture.

The first charter school was organized in 1989 and happenings in New Zealand soon became the model constituency for the new educational phenomenon in North America. Having come to the conclusion that public schooling could be refined and improved by breaking down the standardized approach to teaching and learning, the New Zealand Department of Education mandated all school jurisdictions to develop charter schools to deregulate government educational services. A few years later several states in the United States followed suit; Minnesota was first, followed by California. In 1994 the Province of Alberta also passed a law to permit the establishment of charter schools. Other nations have since taken up the cause, making charter schools an international phenomenon.

Charter schools are usually initiated by special interest groups, parent groups, entrepreneurs or charismatic educational leaders. Sometimes they are even begun by teacher groups. Nathan (1998) contends that the concept of charter schools originated in the United States twenty-three years ago in New England when a group of teachers approached their local school board to explore a new approach to education. The late Albert Shanker, president of the American Federation of Teachers, then publicized the idea and suggested that any school board could charter a local school board provided the union and teachers agreed. In the late 1980s the City of Philadelphia started a series of schools that could be called schools-within-schools, but they were labelled charter schools. In some instances, teachers and students were assigned to these schools while in other cases the schools were selected by students and teachers. Later this concept was refined and formally installed in Minnesota as a charter school program.

The State of Ohio has in place a cap of 125 charter schools (Ohio calls them community schools), which will be lifted on June 30, 2001, thanks to newly-drafted state legislation. Although Ohio's charter schools receive no state funds for construction, the state legislature has arranged for a ten million dollar fund from which charter schools can draw to erect new buildings. They have also been given the right of first refusal on any school buildings that will be sold. Observers expect that the new regulations will encourage a rapid rise in the formation of new charter schools in Ohio (*Akron Beacon Journal*, May 6, 2001).

Defining Charter Schools

Although the concept of charter schools is relatively new, several distinguishing features of this form of education are rapidly emerging. Contreras (1995) has identified a series of characteristics unique to charter schools, suggesting that they are a truly different alternative to schooling, more so than anything that has previously been attempted. Charter schools are not primarily organized by state or local school boards, but by groups of concerned parents or other interest groups. Once a plan for such a school has been drawn up, it is submitted to the local board or state department of education for approval. The proposal to begin a charter school must outline methods of assessment and accountability in the true spirit of decentralization and on-site management. The local body that drew up the charter can form or establish a governing body for the school with the power to revoke or renew the charter if at any point the school fails to meet its student outcome objectives. Charter schools generally receive funding directly from the state as if they are school districts, and the charter school board is accountable for its dissemination because it holds decision-making powers.

Charter schools are not supposed to discriminate deliberately against students. This means that they cannot choose their students on the basis of their backgrounds or other characteristics like academic standing. In practice, however, preference is sometimes given to students with special needs, at least in some of the original schools. When the State of Colorado initiated charter schools, for example, it was mandated that of the first 50 such schools begun, at least 13 should focus on at-risk youth and their special needs. The State of Minnesota permitted only eight charter schools to be established in the whole state, and of those eight schools, five were to offer specific programs for groups such as inner city or hearing disabled.

California regulations pertaining to charter schools are quite specific. These schools are seen as potentially innovative and designed with flexibility in mind in order to better accommodate student needs. In attempting to meet this challenge charter schools are free to design their own curricula, personnel practices, and admission and suspension requirements within certain limits. They have some flexibility in student enrollment, though their student body is to reflect the makeup of the district in which they operate.

They must give preference to students in their attendance area, but they are also allowed to set admission standards so that they may accept students regardless of their district of residence (Becker, et al., 1997).

When New Zealand took a flying leap into the unknown by mandating charter schools with a uniform national curriculum for the entire country, school boards were set up to regulate each local school. In order to affirm the principle of parental governance, members of school boards outnumbered school staff. At the secondary school level there was even provision for student representation on the governing board. Each local school had its own charter outlining its mission statement made up of educational aims, and objectives and targets, and drawn up between the local board and the government. Local school boards were charged by the central government to deliver on their stated aims.

The New Zealand decision to adopt a national curriculum was based on several reasons (McGee, 1995). The state wanted to assure a sound general education for all of its children and at the same time mandated a uniform curriculum in order to assure equal access to training in needed skills and ideas. Geographic mobility was also to be limited by this arrangement. If curricular revision became necessary, it could be universally mandated through the issuance of a single duplicated memo. In this way the central government felt it had fulfilled its commitment to provide equality in its educational delivery system. Periodic checks by school inspectors were intended to assure that program quality was being maintained.

In Canada generally and in Alberta specifically, a charter school may be defined as an autonomous public or separate school designed to make improvements in student learning. It may have a specific purpose or provide a special service. It can be operated by an incorporated society, a company or a provincial corporation. In Alberta, charter schools must be open to all students defined by the legislature to be the kind of clientele who could benefit from the program offered. The schools cannot charge tuition fees, they must be non-sectarian, and they must employ certified teachers. Charter schools are funded at a level comparable to other public schools and are subject to provincial standards and testing. Curriculum may be chosen by parents and teachers, but the program of study must be laid out in the charter or by agreement with the Alberta Department of Education. The provincial government has attempted to depoliticize the charter school phenomenon by maintaining an arms-length approach to the administration and governance of charter schools while maintaining a centralist position in terms of funded, mandated curriculum (Bosetti, 2000: 183).

Statistics regarding the number of charter schools in the United States indicate that as of January 1998, nearly 800 were in operation, enrolling over 170 000 students. Twenty-nine states and the District of Columbia had authorized the establishment of charter schools and President Clinton called for the formation of 3 000 charter schools by the decade's end (Manno, et al., 1998a). Charter schools in America come in all flavors and sizes, some having as few students as fifty and others with enrollments up to a thousand students. The curricula in these schools also vary ranging from traditional to innovative or a mixture of both.

Charter School Claims

Manno, et al. (1998b) claim that charter schools spring from the impulse to meet educational needs that are not being fulfilled in public systems. According to a two-year study financed by the Hudson Institute's Educational Excellence Network, charter schools shift authority from producers to consumers, from experts to laity. They offer diversity in education and feature accountable, results-oriented, professional institutions. Charter schools are usually smaller than conventional public schools and more firmly anchored in local communities. They also emphasize educational specialties which conventional public schools are not able to provide.

Hirsch (1996) has deduced that charter schools gained a following because parents were disillusioned with public education in its traditional form. Instead of producing promised results in academic achievement, constituents were barraged with slogans like critical thinking, individualized instruction, higher-order reasoning, school restructuring and site-based decision-making. Charter schools promised a radical departure from past ways and the band-wagon was soon loaded with passengers. Believing that parent power and local representation would highlight the development of charter schools, in a few short years they gleefully witnessed swelled enrollment figures beyond predicted levels.

By 1996, it became evident that parental choice in education had not greatly improved student achievement in the United States, a result consistent with international evidence gleaned from countries that had developed similar models for public education. In a California study, Becker et al. (1997) made note of small differences in achievement on the part of charter school students when compared with students in other schools, but they attributed these small gains to the fact that the students came from "parent-involved" families. As Hirsch (1996: 61), noted, students in the Netherlands actually showed a decline in achievement levels despite the fact that the country had many years of experience in a school model featuring publicly-funded choice. The conclusion seems to be that public choice of itself is not a sufficient base for school reform.

The underlying philosophical rationale for initiating charter schools is that these schools guarantee a degree of flexibility in the public system through the development of theme schools (Evans et al., 1999). Charter schools are in fact public schools except that each school is encouraged to develop a flavor of its own. Charter schools remain part of the public system but are given greater autonomy to define their own educational mandate in terms of making decisions about staffing, resource allocation, and instructional approaches. They also try to incorporate parental concerns by relating to their local constituency. As a result students at a particular charter school may not necessarily live in the immediate area as might be the case with regular public schools.

Bosetti (2000) has observed that Alberta's ten charter schools are not noted for fostering innovation, but rather seem to fulfil the option of providing choice for parents. In essence, Alberta's charter schools have become a marginalized alternative in public education that has effectively addressed the needs of a few special interest groups. Contreras (1995: 226) describes Charter schools as unfocussed with plenty of opportunity for abuses.

Parents and community groups who favor charter schools often like to claim that these institutions encourage and in fact increase parental involvement in school ongoings. The notion is that of local ownership; when parents feel that they have a say in the control of their school, they are more apt to attend committee meetings pertaining thereto. Parental involvement has been a surprisingly prominent feature of many charter school proposals, particularly in California where state legislation mandates that parents be involved in the governance of such schools. In many of these schools parental involvement is much greater than just helping their children with their homework. Parents are seen as full-scale school assistants who have the interests of all the students in mind, not just their own children. One charter school specifically demands that parents commit themselves to at least two hours of school service per month, and the arrangement is cemented by written contract. If the contract is not honored, the student's registration becomes null and void and the student is expelled (Becker et al., 1997).

There are several reasons why parent involvement in charter schools is higher than in comparison schools, the first being that the enrollment contract commits parents to spending a certain portion of their time in said schools. Another reason may be that charter schools are still a fairly new phenomenon and thus attract the adrenalin flow of enthusiasm more so than traditional schools do. These schools also tend to be smaller in size, thus allowing for a quicker development of a sense of community. If traditional public schools could put as much energy into this aspect of operation as charter schools do, there would surely be a surprising increase in parental involvement as well. Other factors that contributed to increased parental involvement included setting up a parents' lounge, sending home an atypical number of informative school newsletters, and making visits to the homes of involved families in an effort to keep parents interested. Whitty et al. (1998) discovered that while there may have been slightly more parental involvement in charter school ongoings in the schools they studied, it was not necessarily related to the key issues of governance or the nature of curriculum. Becker et. al., (1997) discovered that the literature on parent involvement in charter schools generally supports its importance in building a school community. However, in using parent participation in building community, an unintended side-effect might be that schools can alienate or penalize parents who fail to meet the expectations for involvement. As a result social class and ethnic differences may evolve by eliminating or excluding less-involved families from attending schools where expectations for involvement become codified.

Criticisms

In 1994 the Alberta Teachers' Association took a firm stand against charter schools at its annual representative assembly. The list of objections to charter schools formulated by the association imply that these schools could clearly produce an inequitous situation in the province. Among the concerns of the ATA were that charter schools might exclude students on some basis that could violate human rights legislation or because of the economic or social circumstances of their parents. For example, charter schools could claim the right to remove students for purported violations of a special agreement and deny further responsibility for those students. Those students would then have to be admitted to public schools. The association expressed concern that charter school proponents might admit only students with higher levels of ability or achievement and recruit students by offering financial or other incentives not generally available to students in public schools (Buski, 1995).

One of the fundamental criticisms of charter schools is that they foster an undue amount of competition. This is partly due to the fact that charter schools in North America originated on the basis of fostering choice in schooling. That principle has sometimes been attributed to families who value competitiveness, individualism and achievement, all of which, if projected to the extreme, potentially rupture the relationship between school and community. Bosetti (2000:187) suggests that these charter schools have sometimes been designated as "little fiefdoms catering to the interests of their own social, ethnic, or cultural group, without concern for the larger good." They serve as a fragmenting factor; instead of bringing the public together, they tend to tear it apart by fostering exclusivity. Carl (1996) contends that the move toward charter schools reflects the trends toward deindustrialization, suburbanization and globalization which are currently manifest on this continent. These trends contribute to the breakdown of the social democratic accord which in turn has eroded urban tax bases and isolated many working class city residents from economic and educational opportunities which the more affluent urban and suburbanite citizens enjoy. The result has been disillusionment with public schooling, particularly in urban areas.

A study on parent involvement in charter schools by Becker et al. (1997) in California revealed a number of ways in which charter schools were able to influence a more select student population. Response to a survey of parents indicated that school management was interested in discouraging some families from enrolling their children over the issue of parent involvement. One family, for example, was informally advised not to apply because it was felt that problems would inevitably arise over parent-involvement expectations. Another family did not complete the admission forms because they did not agree with the school's expectations for parent involvement. One parent voluntarily took a child from the school because he or she did not want to fulfil expected commitments of parent involvement. A student was asked to transfer out because the parents were not willing to commit themselves to the level of involvement expected. Of twenty schools contacted about this issue, nine indicated that events such as the above had occurred. Clearly this process was a means of assuring that only those students would be admitted who were from families who had high parental involvement in school ongoings as a value.

Becker and associates found that another method by which to assure some measure of student selectivity was to request that parents wishing to admit their children for the first time (new students) declare themselves willing to assist with school programs "in requested ways." Public schools generally do not have the luxury of insisting on such specific forms of parental participation, and have to enroll any student who requests admission with the exception of severely disabled students requiring special services which the school is not able to provide. By screening parents in this fashion, charter schools could again ensure that the "right kind" of parents were requesting admission for their children. While this criticism may seem a bit harsh, its validity might be tested by examining the makeup of the student population. If charter schools do not resemble public schools in this regard, it will become obvious that some kind of voluntary selection system is in operation.

Not all charter schools necessarily select students on an unfair basis. An exception is Renaissance Charter School at Irving, Texas which was founded in conjunction with the University of Texas at Arlington. When the school started it bolstered its kinship with local public schools and initiated an open enrollment policy. This meant that any and all students who applied and met the admissions criteria were admitted, regardless of race, creed, gender, national origin or religion. Some similarities to private schools exist, however, like the fact that Renaissance Charter School can decide which students remain enrolled and on what grounds. Like a private school, Renaissance leaders had to generate their own startup funds as well as maintenance costs and general operating costs. Once the school was started, state funds were allotted, but like any private school, Renaissance still faced a loss of funding for operating costs and payroll cuts if it did not achieve enrollment projections (McNeil, 1999).

The State of Massachusetts opened fifteen charter schools in 1995, and the one most allied to a profit-making corporate entity received the most financial assistance (Shamon, 1996). Each school was managed by the charter school trustees and the State Secretary of Education (an executive appointee of the governor). Local school committees, town officials and community groups were assigned no jurisdictional rights in the operation of these schools. Local public school officials argued fruitlessly that charter schools were no different than private schools because charter school trustees were not elected by the democratic process. Critics of the plan complained that while the regular school system crumbled under the weight of extra financing for charter schools, the majority of students in the state would suffer because there was simply not enough money to go around when so much of it was being diverted to private interests.

Status of Teachers

An unresolved issue pertaining to charter schools has to do with the relationship of charter schools to teachers' unions. This is of concern since local charter school boards have been assigned fairly comprehensive mandates to run their schools the way they want. This includes the dissemination of funds, and so there have been instances where lower salaries have been paid teachers in charter schools. As employees of charter schools teachers have the right to organize and bargain collectively, but their bargaining unit may have to be separate from that of the school district in which the charter school is located. Such action immediately diminishes the power of a teachers' union in seeking to represent teachers on a larger scale. There is also the related problem of teachers trying to transfer from a charter school into the larger public system since in some instances charter schools are perceived as interlopers on the educational scene. This perspective could affect teachers' opportunities to transfer from one situation to another.

Haché (1999) has summarized the research literature on the New Zealand experiment to suggest that its school reform has been especially hard on teachers. The research shows a very high price in terms of human costs; teachers and principals in New Zealand have revealed a high level of stress, a desire to leave the profession, and a decline in job satisfaction and morale. In many urban centres in New Zealand teachers found themselves working for principals hired from the industrial sector with no training in pedagogy. These administrators were business managers by training and experience who foisted new duties, longer hours and modified roles on the teaching staff.

Charter schools in Massachusetts are not bound by union contracts and teachers need not be certified by the state to teach. As Shamon (1996) points out, the same state educational reform law that established charter schools also raised teacher certification standards. The new requirements do not apply to charter schools, and teachers in those schools can now expect to work without job security for less money and without benefits. The Alberta Teachers' Association expresses a similar concern when noting that charter schools can engage members of staff under agreements that are not subject to collective bargaining and employ teachers who are not active members of a teachers' union (Buski, 1995).

The above would seem to suggest that if the energy and financing had gone into the public system that the charter school movement drained, there would be little cause to complain about the effectiveness of public schools in the western world.

Eight
Public Education for the 21st Century

If alternative froms of public education cannot deliver the goods any better than the institution they were designed to replace, what hope is there to improve the system we have? The answer rests on very optimistic grounds; if the energy and financing that have been devoted to tearing down the public system could be redirected to improving public schools, the dramatic effects of reform could be felt almost overnight.

It would also be of great assistance if national leaders and the body politick could walk the talk in terms of how important education really is. Billions of dollars can so easily be raised for professional sports, for example, even when the resultant scenario basically depicts highly-paid grown men beating each other over the head with a hockey stick or running across a field with an inflated pig bladder tucked under an armpit. If any threat arises that the team may move out of town, the community goes wild. While this reality persists all too often, on the other hand it seems to be well-spent money to pay a minimally-educated, hardly qualified (there are few qualifications for the job), individual a few dollars an hour to provide for the early socialization of the nation's children in a daycare. Do North Americans care enough for quality public education that they will divert funds from professional sports and entertainment towards improving the schools? That is the sixty-four dollar question, but the answer is all too obvious. In the meantime, those who allegedly do care about better schools for the nation's young have unwittingly opted for the alternative of dismantling the public school system in favor of building little walled communities of learning.

The most pressing need in education today is not the right of each individual to free education, but the necessity for a democratic society to provide it and insist upon it. This principle is neither new nor novel, but it is now more urgent than ever. In modern times, every nation charged with the promotion of national welfare and the direction of national policies has tried to provide an education thought to be adapted to the needs of the particular society and the type of government in operation. Both Canada and the United States are committed to the principles of democracy and the notion of a gradual evolution of society and social institutions. Therefore the demands of education in both countries are not less, but greater in terms of trying to educate a citizenry who will be able to adjust to constantly changing economic, scientific and social conditions. Future citizens will need to be educated to be able to participate fully in decision-making that will affect the direction and speed of change. As Lord Henry Peter Broughton once stated in the British House of Commons, "Democratic education should develop citizens who are "easy to lead, but difficult to drive; easy to govern, but impossible to enslave" (Ehlers, 1973: 4). The public school alone is able to deliver on these counts since all other forms of schooling, being largely antithetical in purpose, have private agendas. It behooves every democratic nation, therefore, to maintain a universal form of democratic education for all of its citizens. The approach of the charter school movement augurs against this objective in that it atomizes the public education system into smaller political entities, that is, individual schools as opposed to districts. Thus the isolation and separation of poor communities from each other and from resource-rich communities is exacerbated. This reality makes it very difficult for members of lower socio-economic communities to build coalitions based on mutual interests with people who have the political and economic clout to invent public services such as schools. Wells et al. (1999: 196) note, for example, that "Blacks are the only ones to benefit from resources allocated to the ghetto – and are the only ones harmed when resources are removed – which makes it difficult for them to find partners of political coalitions."

Schools are not the only places in which one can learn, of course. Anyone can readily gain access to information from a myriad of international cities and hideaway places through various forms of media, and even correspond with people in those locations via e-mail. Of course not everyone can visit other countries and benefit from their heritage, culture and lifestyle, but that same source of enrichment is often available at or near one's doorstep. Information notwithstanding, however, there is no substitute for "being there." This statement has as much relevance to daily classroom interactions as it does for visits to exotic places around the world. There is no substitute for the laboratory experience of a public school classroom and anyone who has been educated in an alternative setting could reveal some rough social edges.

Multicultural Concerns

It is estimated that thirty percent of American citizens may be identified as ethnic minorities, many of them having recently arrived from such countries as southeast Asia, Latin America and the Caribbean. Between 1820 and 1970, more than 45 million immigrants, mostly from European countries, entered the United States. In Canada the composite of ethnic minorities constitutes about one-third of the country's population. Many people who migrated to North America in the last century brought with them elements of their homeland traditions, beliefs and practices, many of which are still quite visible today. On arrival here they built schools and churches, established businesses, and integrated with mainstream society in varying degrees of integration. Both Canada and the United States have long prided themselves on being receptive to needy people, immigrants and refugees and both countries have more recently been much more encouraging to these groups to maintain their cultural identities after they have established themselves.

Two decades ago Tiedt and Tiedt (1979) announced that the outdated melting pot theory of the United States was dead. From the time of the Declaration of Independence in 1776 till near the end of the last century it was popular in the United States to believe that America was God's crucible. Those already settled in the New Land believed that everyone else who came to the United States wanted to be an American in the fullest sense of the word. As multiculturalism gained roots and spawned down south the melting pot theory became inadequate and cultural diversity came to be recognized as a strength, not a weakness. Today many ethnocultural communities in the United States are responding favorably to the opportunities of multiculturalism and have worked hard to maintain their cultural identities, including their customs, beliefs and language. As Baines et al. (1999: 23) suggest,

> Despite the calamities of the past 30 years, public schools are amongst the most steadfastly democratic institutions in the world. They are the only places left where all ethnicities, religions, competencies, and castes are joined together in common purpose.

Sadly, private schools are not diversifying at the rate that public schools are, thereby limiting their role as multicultural institutions (Proweller, 1999). Charter school reform can also lead to further divisions across racial and ethnic groups within inner-city areas. Wells et al. (1999) confirmed this in their California study. In one urban district a group of Latino parents and educators struggled to form a school within the public system that would centre on Latino cultural history and culture. In the process they separated themselves from other ethnocultural communities in the same school district. Lacking funding, the end result was relative deprivation in terms of resources, equipment and supplies. Meanwhile, a nearby suburban charter school was flooded with new technology and instructional materials. This example substantiates the reality that any hope for reducing racism lies in large part within a good public school system (MacEwan, 1996: 10).

It may be old hat to say so, the world is getting smaller and a global outlook is a virtual necessity nowadays. Moreover, it is an international reality. McNergney et al. (1997) studied multicultural contexts in five selected world locations including Singapore, India, South Africa, England and Denmark in an effort to identify related themes, structures and strategies. The conclusion was that leaders in these nations were aware of the necessity to incorporate multicultural concerns in institutional contexts to prepare future generations to be able to function effectively in both global and local societies. This reality cannot be overemphasized since people around the world are increasingly recognizing the global context within which their local actions take place.

Cultural Diversity in the United States

The plea for recognition of the advantages of cultural diversity was actually made by philosopher, Horace Kallin (1882-1974), at the turn of the 20th century. Kallin arrived in America from Poland but saw the opportunity for a degree of cultural integrity in the New Land. He argued strongly against assimilation, insisting that one could be a good American citizen while practicing a slightly different, albeit valid, form of cultural lifestyle (Kallin, 1924). Earlier, another philosophical pioneer, Jane Addams (1990), established Hull House in Chicago in 1899 and opened it as a halfway-house, learning centre, and educational institution for immigrants and families trapped without minimal literacy on the lower steps of the nation's socio-economic ladder. She protested against the treatment of immigrants in sweatshops and worked to get labor laws changed to protect their interests (Miller-Lachmann and Taylor, 1995). It was not until the protest movements of the 1960s, including civil rights, women's liberation, Black power, and opposition to the Vietnam War, that these ideas were afforded widespread attention (Gay, 1983). Gradually government policy began to reflect the national feeling that it was acceptable for individuals and groups to maintain their cultural heritages and not try to deny or hide them or be ashamed of them. Along with this development was the encouraged shift to new expectations of public tolerance and acceptance of unique cultural lifestyles. Cultural pluralism is even being touted as a healthy national composition, but not necessarily to the extent of heightening ethnic group identity to the point of causing fragmentation or intergroup antagonism as is sometimes charged. According to some observers, multiculturalism is widely viewed as a developing national policy (Bennett, 1990; Gay, 1992).

Putting multiculturalism into practice is more than a mild challenge because of such factors as its vague definitions, lack of government funding, and a scarcity of reliable academic studies that support and substantiate multicultural claims. As it is, too many writers who tried to validate the approach or have defended it a bit too strongly ended up promoting a kind of academic ghettoization (Grant and Millar, 1992). Another difficulty has been the charge that multiculturalism is probably just another recently-innovated social movement that could pass from memory even before its impact is felt nationally. House (1992) suggests that like multiculturalism, nationalism too, is a fairly new player on the international scene. Its quick spring to acceptance was spurred on in part by printed languages. When cheap newsprint became available, many speakers of the vernacular also became readers for the first time. People began imagining themselves as members of a much larger community than their local group and at the height of its intensity, their feelings of nationalism even drove them to become willing to give their lives for their nation.

The challenge of formulating a functional mix of multiculturalism with the democratic process often produces tensions with national implications. As Gordon (1964) has emphasized, when pluralism is encouraged, questions quickly arise pertaining to the extent to which separatism can be practiced without risk to the general national welfare.

If culturally divergent groups are awarded the right to preserve the basic elements of their lifestyle, at what point does this arrangement interfere with the rights of others? To what extent does the existence and practice of cultural separateness contribute towards the welfare of the nation as a whole? Gordon uses the phrase "good and reasonableness" in this context as though to imply that any measure of cultural contributions and the recognition of rights should be enacted in an atmosphere of reason and good will.

Gordon's good intentions notwithstanding, critics of multiculturalism have been quite vocal about their fears that such a policy of divergency produces a country that is hard to govern because of the difficulties in informing and maintaining functional political coalitions. Multiculturalism has also been viewed as a hindrance to national unity, an approach that magnifies differences, and, in fact, functions as only a sop to ethnocultural communities. These groups are appeased by the apparent cultural value of the policy when in essence its programs exist only to placate them (Friesen, 1993b).

A democratic society, by definition, is committed to discussion and debate of relevant issues pertaining to, among other things, national destiny. In a democratic society, even the definition of democracy is open to discussion. Of course the dominant group in a democracy will set limits to individual and group behavior, and define the parameters of what will be labelled "normative" behavior, but minorities have both the right and obligation to resist. There are many examples of violations of societal norms, often enacted by minority groups of good will trying to practice what they deem to be inalienable rights. Yet, democracies can be exceedingly tolerant and liberal. A case in point is that of the Amish in America whose once illegal, private one-room country schools were approved by Supreme Court Action in 1972 on the basis that the Amish were not hurting anyone by maintaining their own schools (Friesen, 1983; Friesen and Friesen, 1996).

Canadian Multiculturalism

Multiculturalism has been viewed differently in Canada than in the United States. When Americans adopt a new national policy, they tend to be quite open and even brash about it. Canadians, on the other hand, are more reserved, even though the notion of a cultural mosaic has pretty well always been a national policy, at least in written form. A Canadian sociologist, John Porter, once defined Canadians as conservative and authoritarian and more oriented to tradition, hierarchy, and elitism in the sense of showing deference to those in high status, and united in defense of these values against the egalitarianism and aggressiveness of American culture (Porter, 1987).

The Canadian multicultural mix was highlighted around the turn of the last century when the nation's population suddenly skyrocketed by 43 percent, making the immigrant population rise to 22 percent of the nation's whole. In 1911, people of non-British and non-French origins formed 34 percent of the population of Manitoba, 40 percent of the population of Saskatchewan, and 33 percent of the population of Alberta. There were early signs that the assimilation process was not completely effective in that arriving immigrants were not being absorbed into the mainstream. National leaders could not explain why this was so, partially because their own ethnocentrism blocked their view. A key factor in hindering assimilation was the nature of designed block settlements which allowed immigrant groups to live together and to practice their traditional lifestyles free from outside influences. In effect this was also an excellent vehicle by which ethnocultural communities could develop into what critics called "little islands of secluded empires" (Friesen, 1993b: 6).

By World War I the intensification of the assimilation process reached new heights as hyphenated Canadians were ferreted out for discrimination. German-speaking immigrants were forbidden to speak their language and a series of negative stereotypes pertaining to Asian immigrants originated. Although Canadians in the various regions reacted a bit differently to this scenario, a particular pattern could be identified in the west. As Palmer (1982: 180) noted, it was only after the conclusion of the First World War that ". . .each province saw the growth of greater tolerance generated by new social, economic and intellectual conditions."

After the Second World War ended, it took the nation some time to adjust to its aftermath. The arrival of many intellectuals among the postwar refugees from eastern Europe, coupled with an enhanced motivation for upward mobility among second and third generation resident AngloCanadians, forced the issue of inequality out into the open. Increased intermarriage and residential dispersion also worked to break down traditional racial and cultural barriers. Thus the period of the 1950s grew to be called "the quiet cultural revolution" as the demand for greater government recognition on the part of newer ethnic groups mounted.

The good news of Canadian multiculturalism occurred in the 1960s, a time when both Canada and the United States were in a state of social and political unrest. On December 17, 1962, the Canadian federal government appointed a Royal Commission on Bilingualism and Biculturalism for the purpose of enquiring into a reporting on the existing state of bilingualism and biculturalism in the country. In 1970 the commission recommended that Canada commit herself to two official languages and two official cultures, but the government was not prepared for the nation's response to this proposal. Many ethnic groups were chagrined to discover that their heritages were not seen to be on par with those of the English and French Charter Nations and nothing was to be done about their perpetuation. Aboriginal peoples were a bit annoyed that the English and French were allotted the title of Founding Nations when indeed there had been nations and cultures in existence in Canada long before the so-called Charter Nations arrived.

Amidst the uproar, and in an effort to please everyone, on October 8, 1971, Prime Minister Pierre Elliott Trudeau arose in the House of Commons to declare an official national policy of bilingualism and multiculturalism. The new policy was committed to recognizing the variety of heritage cultures resident in the nation and the government indicated its intent to assist the members of all cultural groups to overcome barriers to full participation in Canadian society. In addition, the federal government would encourage and assist the development of different cultural groups who have demonstrated such a desire and encourage these groups to promote interchange with other ethnocultural groups. Bilingualism remained a federal goal but the government committed itself to assisting immigrants in acquiring facility in at least one of the two official languages. As it turned out, it remained mainly the responsibility of public schools to translate these objectives into forms of daily interaction.

Within a year or two of the passing of federal legislation on multiculturalism, the various provinces enacted legislation or determined related policies. Manitoba offered the first positive response to the challenge, passing a form of related legislation a year later. Ontario established an Advisory Council on Multiculturalism in 1973, but Quebec, Prince Edward Island and Newfoundland refused to do so. Quebec argued that a policy on "intercultural education" was more suitable, and Newfoundland and Prince Edward Island insisted that they had no need for a multicultural policy.

Schooling on the Frontline

While North American governments were wrestling with relevant policy-making in multiculturalism, educators were busy trying to operationalize the new movement. In 1976, Margaret Gibson offered a breakdown of the efforts of educators to spell out in practice what the implications of cultural diversity were for that time (Gibson, 1976). Gibson identified four models for the delivery of multicultural programs including: (i) education of the culturally different; (ii) education about cultural differences; (iii) education for cultural pluralism; and, (iv) bicultural education. Gibson suggested that the first option was clearly assimilative in intent and targeted people newly arriving in North America where many thought they would "have to be assimilated." The underlying assumption of this approach was that the cultural stance of incoming groups was inferior to that of the established society and they would have to make the necessary adjustments.

The second option, education about cultural differences aimed at developing cultural sensitivity and understanding by examining the history, beliefs and lifestyles of cultural groups other than one's own. The approach basically consisted of case studies of selected ethnocultural communities, preferably those with whom students would have some measure of contact. Critics of the idea suggested that case studies frequently centred on the "food, fun, festivals and finery" elements of studied cultures without gaining much appreciation for the deeper meanings within each configuration. It was also suggested that since the school had an underlying assimilative intent, the study of other cultures was meant to yield little more than a curious look.

This criticism is fundamentally unfair since public schools generally bend over backwards to accommodate religious and cultural nuances. In fact, the current trend in Canada is to eliminate anything smacking of a Christian theme (Christmas, Easter, etc.) in public schools lest anyone migrating to this country be offended about the celebration of the nation's history. On the other hand, teachers are often overly concerned with injecting other cultural holiday emphases (sacred or otherwise) into the curriculum even if only to show how broadminded they have become. Sadly, this means that the nation's own historical development is ignored at the expense of more international concerns. Perhaps in the future it will be possible to balance the account by making newcomers feel at home at the same time as acquainting them with the nation's historical development.

Private and parochial schools with a distinct religious base probably have a reverse problem of sorts. Instead of being able to view alternate religious interpretations of the universe as equally valid to their own, they will find it necessary to indicate why their own metaphysical perspective is superior to all others. This tack may establish students' minds firmly within the parameters of the desired forms of thought, but it could certainly straitjacket their thinking later on when they may have opportunities to delve deeper into the examination of other world philosophies. Too often the student body of non-public schools are singular in religious and cultural makeup, thereby shortchanging students of the opportunity to rub shoulders with people of varying views and lifestyles with any degree of meaning. It is one thing to study other cultural configurations, and quite another to be in a situation where one's classmates represent a wide range of cultural and philosophical backgrounds.

Gibson's third approach fares little better than the second, since school environments are hardly capable of educating for cultural pluralism with any far-reaching consequences. It would take more influence than the school is capable of to achieve any degree of success in a domain that affects all of the basic structures of society including business, politics, religion, economics, and the like. Implicit in this approach is the belief that the state has the responsibility of helping all ethnic groups to preserve their heritage languages and cultures. Schools employing this approach may attempt to enhance harmonious relations among their various ethnocultural sectors by means of curriculum emphases, exchange visits and collaboration. The efficacy of this approach will be directly linked to the multicultural makeup of the school population.

Gibson's final approach to teaching multiculturalism is called "biculturalism," and it implies that learners be educated to be able to function with equal ease in two distinctly different cultural contexts – usually that of dominant society and that of their home culture. It is questionable whether or not any individual can function equally well in two entirely different contexts because the challenge may lead to a form of cultural schizophrenia or cultural marginality. The end result of such an arrangement could be that individuals would learn to function quite effectively in both contexts, but end up being truly at home in neither.

An illustrative scenario pertains to individuals raised in very restrictive environments (like Hutterites or Amish, for example), and, on leaving their particular cultural enclave, may discover that there is another world out there with which they are not ready to cope. After considerable time spent struggling with the challenge, they may eventually discover a degree of ease in functioning in dominant society, only to find that they no longer fit altogether into the milieu of their home culture. This same situation can occur when individuals have been enrolled in a restrictive or exclusive private school or in a home school context and they are then "released" into society. They may discover that people think differently "out there," and they may actually learn to like it. This discovery may result in their being frustrated, even to the point of being angry at those who kept them philosophically in the dark.

The Global Concern

Ouellet (1992) has outlined four options for selecting an approach to teaching multiculturally, three of which parallel Gibson's delineation of education of the culturally different (assimilation), education about cultural differences (cross-cultural education), and education about cultural differences (the multicultural option). Ouellet emphasizes that today's fast-changing and technologically-driven world demands a transcultural perspective which encourages individuals to look beyond their own cultural parameters in an attempt to understand and appreciate those of other groups and nations. It is a very difficult challenge to realize with sincerity that members of cultural groups different from one's own will value their belief system and lifestyle as much as one does one's own, but it is a goal worth striving for. The most likely arena available to young children in which to develop such a sense of appreciation is the public school because its student body will be more widely representative of cultural diversity.

Concern about the need for developing a global outlook grew to a crescendo during the 1980s after multiculturalism had grown respectable. As world travel and increased knowledge of events in other nations became household possibilities, it also became clear that global concerns had become local concerns. Today, any event or operant trend in any part of the world affects everyone and underscores the interrelatedness of all peoples. As anthropologist Margaret Mead put it, "You can no longer save your family, tribe, or nation. You can only save the world" (Bennett, 1990: 276). Surely the best place to practice this outlook in early youth is in a public school setting.

The Global Creed

The assumptions on which global education is based are easily accommodated in public schools; in fact, they are a necessary part of the mandate of educating the nation's young. In the first instance, public schools must be accessible to everyone, regardless of race, creed or color. Public school classrooms must provide an environment in which all students can recognize their origins and cultural backgrounds as assets. They must be able to see themselves as worthwhile human beings, not in spite of their unique attributes, but because of them. Students should be able to interact positively with their peers in the classroom, freely bringing their total identities (beliefs, culture, lifestyle, etc.), to bear on the learning situation. They should be able to attack meaningful learning tasks with an expectation of insights and abilities, they should at the same time recognize that the cultural backgrounds of others in the classroom are also valuable aspects of a pluralistic society (Friesen, 1993b: 75).

It must be difficult to exercise the above creed in a school setting with specific philosophical parameters such as that of an exclusive private school. Obviously this would not be a value in such a context. Private schools often make the same claims, it is true, but when chips are down, in some private schools there simply cannot be more than minimal tolerance of the beliefs or practices of certain ethnocultural or religious groups. This can be illustrated with reference to the origins of the Kneehill Christian School begun at Linden, Alberta, by the Church of God in Christ, Mennonite (Holdeman) denomination some years ago (Friesen, 1983). The school gained notoriety when the Province of Alberta took the matter to court, charging one parent, Elmer Wiebe, in the supporting Mennonite community. After only two days of trial a verdict of "not guilty" was handed down on February 6, 1978. Judge Oliver ruled that based on the Alberta Bill of Rights the rights of parents were not superseded by the Provincial School Act and the Provincial School Act would have to be amended to accommodate the decision. The school act was therefore changed, the Kneehill Christian School became legal, and Elmer Wiebe was exonerated.

A new category of school came into existence as a result of the trial of the Kneehill Christian School. Now it was possible to operate a school in the province that chose its own curriculum, and did not necessarily hire certified teachers, but was still subject to periodic inspection on behalf of the state. In addition, the school would not be eligible for any public funding. As it happened, the school did not use provincially-designed curriculum, but instead imported materials from Ontario and from the United States designed by an Amish group. School inspectors were a bit concerned about the fact that Holdeman students were learning about the fifty American states, the United States Congress and Senate and the presidential office instead of learning about the ten Canadian provinces governed by a prime minister. Of greater concern was the nature of the curriculum content.

In one instance, for example, a caption under a picture of a Hindu man praying to a wooden statue read, "This man is praying to a god who cannot help" (Friesen, 1983: 90). Although pressure was put on Holdeman educators to eliminate such illustrations in their curricula, there can be little doubt that the incident was consistent with Holdeman beliefs and something they wanted their children to endorse as well. As fundamental Christians their belief system would not expand to the point that they would possibly conceive of any advantage to be gained by offering prayers to anyone else but the God in whom they (the Holdeman People) believed. Clearly this approach would be difficult to justify under the auspices of any global education program.

Five Steps to a Global Outlook

The literature which fosters cross-cultural appreciation as a means of promoting national good will reveals that the process is not uncomplicated (Fleras and Elliott, 1992; Garcia, 1994: Gollnick and Chinn, 1986; Ghosh, 1996). It is necessary to begin with the premise that no one can help being born who they are. No one chooses their physical shape or size, race, belief system or culture or personal identity. These characteristics are accidents of birth and no one should rightly ever be blamed or credited for having them.

A second necessary condition to grasping a global outlook is to believe that nearly everyone gains some measure of appreciation for their heritage and background as they grow up, and this is understandable. The third condition is probably impossible to ask of everyone and certainly not a feasible request of educators operating within an educational setting that fosters a specific creed. The bottom line is to understand that what others believe is as important to them as what we believe is to us. An even further step would be to endorse what others believe as equally valid in the human universe of thought. A breakdown of this model may be elaborated in a crescendo of intensity featuring five steps: (i) tolerance, (ii) understanding, (iii) acceptance, (iv) appreciation, and, (v) affirmation.

1. Tolerance

The road of least effort in so far as attempting to understand culture configurations other than one's own is merely to put up with them. This is the meaning of tolerance. This stance requires no energy other than awareness, which of itself could happen accidentally. There is no requirement to accommodate anyone; at best, the effort is simply a form of tokenism (Baruth and Manning, 1992; Miller-Lauchmann and Taylor, 1995). Tolerance can be patronizing, and often emanates from a strong feeling of ethnocentrism because it implies a position of superiority on the part of those doing the tolerating (Elliott and Fleras, 1992). Tolerance per se implies no obligation for adjustment and no need for further learning. It is a dead-end street and does not even deserve a passing grade in terms of strengthening any links of human communication. Any school program can teach tolerance in the sense that the existence of other cultures and belief systems is acknowledged. There is no further movement to learn anything about these configurations with a possible view to appreciating their distinctiveness.

2. Understanding

A slightly deeper level of cultural sensitivity emanates from the effort to understand, to cognitively become aware of different meanings, or varying interpretations of the workings of the universe, for example. With this stance energy is devoted to understanding perspectives; why do people behave the way they do? Why do certain ethnocultural groups believe so strongly in their unique religious enactments? Why do some religious groups believe in specific rules, taboos or sanctions?

Cultural understanding takes time and effort; it takes time to walk in someone else's shoes or moccasins, to study other lifestyles and value systems and social structures. When this tack is undertaken, the road to cultural understanding will allow some measure of effective intercultural communication to occur. Both parties in the process will find it possible to move towards the other in a cognitive sense.

The fundamental plank of schooling is curriculum, namely the materials that are studied by students throughout their sojourn in that institution. Naturally the selection of materials is important and should be made on the basis that it represents a fair cross-section of the foundational knowledge of society. Schools have an obligation to introduce students to the data base on which they will later be making adult decisions. This is particularly true of public schools which have an obligation to provide such a foundation for all future citizens. Schools other than public, be they private, parochial or home schools, do not have this obligation as a first premise. Their first priority is to inculcate their students in the rudiments of the creed which separates them from the rest of society. Thus their primary objective may be credal, philosophical or even spiritual, depending on the modus operandi of the particular school. These schools, because of their lack of obligation to society, cannot be harnessed with the responsibility of socializing the young to fit into mainstream society. In fact, in many instances, the promoters of these schools have no such intention. As will later be seen, this reality may influence students to develop only limited appreciation for diversity.

3. Acceptance

The mode of acceptance implies coming to terms with something such as a belief, behavior or happening. Most social scientists are probably agreed that there are significant cultural differences among cultures, and the members of each cultural configuration have what they consider valid reasons for behaving the way they do. When students of human behavior cognitively understand why people behave the way they do, there is still another step that can be taken toward fuller understanding, namely to accept the proffered rationale. It is one thing to understand a given belief, enactment or process, but it is quite another thing personally to be "O.K." with the proffered reason for its practice. To make peace with the explanation requires a deeper comprehension and a conscious motivation to incorporate or inculcate that rationale into one's own modus operandi. People can understand that there are different ways of doing things or different ways of explaining the "same" phenomena, but to accept that these alternate explanations are as valid as those which they personally endorse requires extraordinary effort.

4. Appreciation

To appreciate something requires much more effort than just being aware of or tolerating that particular belief or behavior. The act of appreciating something means recognizing the value of it, thinking well of it, or esteeming it. This stance is quite far removed from knowing that members of a specific cultural configuration do things a certain way; it is the act of finding value in the way they do it. Any society with specific ways of doing most things can be quite ethnocentric, and most of its members will probably not be too willing to give their blessing to what they perceive to be unorthodox, unusual or even "weird" beliefs or behaviors for no good reason other than to be generous. This may be the rub of being a global person – to recognize, study, and understand credal or cultural peculiarities, and once they are understood, commend them for the satisfaction they provide to the people who hold them dear. In pushing the concept to its logical conclusion, it should be mentioned that individuals so convinced might even consider adopting some element of the newly-encountered values for themselves. Such an occurrence could indeed be called cultural appreciation which is a vital plank of any global education program.

With the agenda of providing something for everyone, public schools do not to have to fret about possible value shifts or adoption of new values by students. No matter what the subject matter, be it orthodox, ordinary or controversial, there are always people in some sector of society who will appreciate the various emphases being promoted in school. Controversial topics such as family life and sex education, substance abuse, religion, or values can probably be bypassed or avoided by educators in non-public schools, but unless there is considerable opposition from any sector, the public school experiences no such restrictions. An institution committed to preparing the nation's young for virtually any possible scenario, must constantly dare to launch out onto new ground, regardless of how philosophically precarious it may be. Non-public schools can afford to be cautious in this regard; after all, their obligations are restricted by their constituencies.

5. Affirmation

It was Plato who said it first and probably said it best; the ideal society with a truly global outlook is one in which everyone performs the tasks they are best qualified to perform and everyone is equally valued for his or her contributions. In such a society one could conceivably endorse, encourage and even celebrate the fruits of true diversity (Siccone, 1995). Educationally speaking, it is a well-researched fact that students who receive positive feedback from their teachers perform better than those who are insecure or unsure about themselves (Bennett, 1990; Grant, 1995). Thus it is very important to endorse or affirm every student for who they are if their learning capacities are to be maximized.

Teachers in public schools by nature of their calling are obligated to avoid the use of stereotypes or language that could hurt students' feelings. Public school teachers should employ language that is free of sexist or racist connotations and profile people as having varied characteristics other than just race, sex, religion or ethnic background. Such a mode can open students' eyes to the greater potential of human ingenuity and individuality. Once this reality is introduced it may be possible to develop a classroom atmosphere in which everyone feels physically, psychologically and culturally safe.

The extent to which private school content can be restrictive may be illustrated with reference to an Amish school curriculum designed by Pathway Publishers in Ontario. Legally, the one-room private schools run by the 3 000-plus member Amish community in southern Ontario have not been approved, but the Provincial Department of Education ignores their status. In an effort to restrict the reading materials encountered by children in these schools, the Amish have developed their own textbooks and workbooks with the need to do so based on this observation: "We cannot afford to orally teach them the principles of God's Word, and then turn them lose with books that deny it" (Friesen, 1998: 6). Essentially the curriculum consists of stories, poems and sentences targeted at the language arts with social studies deliberately omitted. That subject matter offers too much opportunity to learn about alternative lifestyles, some of which might be disapproved by the community's spiritual leaders. Values to be appropriated by the students are spelled out in very specific terms. Teachers' guides which accompany these materials are clear, forthright and specific since Amish teachers generally have no formal training beyond eighth grade. It is not unusual to encounter statements such as the following in a teacher's guide (Friesen, 1998: 7, italics mine):

> This story has a lesson, and the teacher must help children get the lesson by discussing the story thoroughly. The children should be led to understand that Rachel could not do as much as she thought she could. . . . Gently, but firmly, *have them do it right.*

The content of Amish school curriculum, which is also widely used in Amish schools in the United States focusses exclusively on the Amish way of life. Most stories read by the students will have to do with farm life, that is, children doing chores like milking, baking, haying, harvesting or cleaning the barn. At the sixth grade level, and in isolated instances before that, children are introduced to aspects of the "outside world" through stories about other countries. One example pertains to the use of St. Bernard dogs in Switzerland where the Amish originated. Several stories are about Anabaptist heroes of faith, and one slightly unrealistic account has to do with a magazine story about millions of people starving to death in India. Awareness of this fact on the part of the family reading it only motivates them to be extra grateful for their own food supply. No attempt is made to apply the lesson to the notion of responsibility for outsiders who may be in difficulty.

Amish schools are probably somewhat unusual in the extent to which they place limitations on the parameters of their school ongoings. Their restrictive approach is a far cry from that of schools in Japan where global education is currently making a breakthrough. Not only are Japanese students learning about the values and customs of other nations, they are also studying aggressive actions taken by the Japanese against other nations. One recent topic was war crimes by the Japanese against other Asian people and the responsibilities that Japan bore for its aggression in that war. The students also investigated the situation in Okinawa where more than 100 000 people were killed after World War II and where suffering continued after the war due to the presence of US military bases (Asano, 2000).

Suffice it to say, these Japanese students were studying in a public school.

Nine
Improving Public Education

Proposals for improving public schooling in the last half century have always been ample in number and scope, and recommended formuli have emanated from individuals and groups representing the entire gamut from professional educators to business leaders to people-on-the street. As critics have persisted in plying their trade, school systems all over the world have continued to expand and change to meet social needs. More than three decades ago Philip Coombs (1968: 4) cautioned that school systems were adapting too slowly to the needs around them, with a consequent disparity between educational systems and their environments. Many would still make that claim. Coombs pointed out that an assorted array of factors contributed to what he termed an educational crisis, including: (i) the sharp increase in popular aspirations for education which is still continuing to lay seige to existing schools and universities; (ii) the acute scarcity of resources which constrained educational systems from responding more fully to new demands; (iii) the inherent inertia of educational systems that caused them to respond too sluggishly in adapting their internal affairs to new external necessities, even when resources have not been the main obstacle to adaptation; and, (iv) the inertia of societies themselves, that is, the heavy weight of traditional attitudes, religious customs, prestige and incentive packages, and institutional structures – which blocked them from making the optimum use of education and of educated manpower to foster national development.

In 1975, an invitational conference called "The Alternative Futures of Education" was sponsored by the Research for Better Schools in Philadelphia featuring nine nationally-known educators and social scientists (Rubin, 1975). Conference participants speculated on changes that would affect the institution by the beginning of the twenty-first century. Now that it is possible to look back on their predictions with an element of realism, it is encouraging to note that some of their prognostications were not that far off. Kenneth Boulding (1975), for example, predicted a heightened demand for education by the year 2000 which has been borne out by rising statistics in both secondary and post-secondary enrollments on this continent. Boulding's rationale for this phenomenon included the proposition that financial support for public schooling would be increased and involve older students in its ranks. During the 1970s it was customary to confine the benefits of education to people under the age of twenty, but, as we have witnessed, this is no longer the case. Boulding also predicted a knowledge explosion that would replace the current stock of knowledge with more technologically-based forms of knowing (Boulding, 1975, 68-69). The current reliance on computer technology has certainly validated this thesis and it shows no signs of abatement.

Myers and Simpson (1998) suggest that public schools be reformatted to a new design based on four dimensions: (i) schools as morally-based communities of learners; (ii) learning as experience-based intellectual construction; (iii) teaching as a professional practice of investigative problems identification and problem-solving; and, (iv) teacher learning as the development of professional knowledge, competence, and values in the context of practice. Schools can become morally-based communities when they are viewed as cultures instead of institutions. As cultures they have a moral purpose, a mission, and a shared set of core values. Their moral purpose is to maximize the learning potential of every student, and their fundamental goal is to engage all students in learning to the highest level. Undoubtedly, most schools already aspire to these objectives, but in learning cultures the mission and goal will be recognized constantly and more forcefully, and both will be used more consistently to create better learning for everyone.

In a school-as-culture model, school management involves all community – administration, students and parents. The scenario is not unlike that of the traditional family farm in which all family members had a role to play. The parents may have decided which crops to plant, but teenagers did the milking, and younger children carried in wood and water and helped shell peas during harvest. All possessed equal loyalty to the enterprise and all benefitted from the farm's annual yields. When the final wheat sheaf was brought in from the field, all celebrated in their mutual endeavor to wrest yet another year's food supply from the elements. In similar vein, participants in a school-as-culture model can share in the joy that universal learning has taken place; it is everyone's responsibility and everyone's celebration. It truly does take a whole village to raise a child.

When learning is viewed as experience-based intellectual construction, the school scene will change dramatically. This approach places the onus for the activity on learners, which is just as it should be. After all, it is their knowledge on which they will be basing future decisions, not the knowledge which their teachers possess. Teachers will need to create learning experiences for students instead of envisaging future graduates as products of a particular stream of activity. This approach may be enriched by perceiving of teaching as an investigative problem-identification and problem-solving enterprise with the onus for learning on both teachers and students. This process will continue throughout the remainder of the student's life.

The public is probably unaware that the professional knowledge which teachers possess is basically the knowledge of practice rather than theory. True, that knowledge will be based on sound theoretical constructs, but it will primarily focus on knowing ways to enhance the learning experiences of students by encouraging them to investigate, analyze and synthesize data for themselves. The best teachers are those who help instill in students' minds the notion that learning per se is a great human privilege and students want very much to be involved in it. This implies that there can be few restrictions on the content of learning to be explored. Of course it helps that teachers have also mastered a degree of subject matter such as language arts, mathematics or social studies, but unless their students develop the urge to master something on their own, all the subject mastery on the part of the teacher will pretty much have been in vein in terms of what we define as teaching. In this sense the most useful professional knowledge that teachers possess is practical rather than theoretical.

Violence in Schools

There are a number of very crucial challenges to be faced by educators and politicians alike if public schools are going to continue to be the dynamic influence they have been on this continent over the past couple of centuries. One of the very basic requirements to improving schools is to make them safe, physically and psychologically safe. Over the past two decades educators have worked hard on the latter part of the mandate, that is, to make classrooms psychologically healthy, while taking for granted that children would not be stabbed or shot to death in those very same classrooms. For some observers the situation has reached uncontrollable proportions.

> . . . Schooling has become a site of both symbolic and physical violence and young people experience this violence in multiple ways. They experience – as both perpetrator and victim – physical violence inside and outside the classroom. They vicariously experience violence in the seductive realms of television, films, and popular culture. They are forced to partake of a schooling system and curriculum that does violence to their psyches. And they exist – most importantly – in a political climate where the terms "youth" and "violence" nearly become synonymous. (Dimitriadis and McCarthy, 1999: 125-126)

In recent years educators have developed workable school-community relations to ensure a psychologically healthy classroom environment for students and teachers. Unfortunately, they have not been helped by the fact that we live in a society fraught with increasing violence everywhere. Crime rates are higher than they were a generation or two ago, and violence is seen as synonomous with professional sports and a valid form of entertainment in the media.

It must be recognized that some students have been indoctrinated to be aggressive in resolving disputes before they come to school and not necessarily by school influences. In such cases teachers will find themselves at odds with the value systems based in some social sectors. In school however, name-calling is out, self-esteem has been addressed and students are successfully being challenged to make everyone feel at home regardless of their race, creed, religion, physical appearance or personal philosophy of life. These frontiers have not been easy to conquer, but they have been necessitated at least in part by the fact that schools today serve as the major institution for maintaining and perpetuating national culture, and communicating the values, beliefs and norms of society. In fact, some recent circuit and district courts have made rulings that open the door to the possibility that school board members and instructional staff have a constitutional duty to protect students from harm (Bittner, 1995).

It is easy to point fingers when things go awry, of course, and eighty percent of Americans perceive violence to be a problem in public schools. It is a harsh truth that 40 000 American children bring guns to school every day and about 1.2 million homes with children store at least one loaded, unlocked gun (*USA Today*, May 9, 2001). In a survey in Canada it was found that eighty percent of those polled felt that there was more violence in schools now than ten years ago (MacDonald, 1997). In 1996 more teachers cited discipline problems over any other problem as the main reason for their leaving the profession (Gorder, 1996; Baines et al., 1999). Recent cases of school violence have attracted reams of criticism of public schooling, many of them quite unfounded. Tirozzi (1999), for example, discovered that at Columbine High School all evidence suggests the presence of a caring and loving community of school administrators, staff members, parents and agencies who were vigilant and focussed on the well-being of the students.

Trump (1998) urges school officials to take critical steps to develop specific safe programs and install security techniques in order to assure the safety of all students. School officials need to comprehend the real school security threats that challenge educators and students, then establish an environment where political concerns will take a backseat to school security. Moreover, students can successfully be taught to resolve disagreements through conflict resolution training (Johnson and Johnson, 1996). When violence does occur, care must be taken to offer support for victims of violence (MacDonald, 1997). These measures must be undertaken with common agreement and in a rational, effective and timely manner.

Trump (1998) has outlined a series of myths about school safety that require a closer look. Seven of the top myths include these gems: *first*, it is widely believed that schools have always had security problems but administrators have sufficient experience to handle these. *Second*, incidents of school violence almost always involve drugs, gangs or related underlying issues. *Third*, bullying is not a significant issue in the "big picture" of school security concerns. *Fourth*, violent student behavior cannot be prevented.

Fifth, students sell drugs only for the money, but school officials are adequately trained to handle drug issues. *Sixth,* there have always been gangs in school but gangs are basically a community problem, not a school problem. *Seventh,* and finally, experienced educators have seen it all; the problems will always be the same, just with different players. All of the above are unsubstantiated and somewhat widely believed myths.

It is obvious from Trump's research that new times bring new crimes. The new crimes are not invented in school as much as they are a reflection of what goes on in society. Young people learn from their elders – and from the media. Just as members of the school and community constituencies have grown more educated and sophisticated over the past few decades, so have the behaviors of those who would work their diabolical havoc in our schools. Some of the newer items on the list of lurking dangers include bomb threats, group conflict related to race or cultural issues, computer-related crimes, sexual harassment and sex crimes such as date rape. As the media have pointed out all too well in recent months, any or all of these crimes (and others) can happen on any playground, or in any classroom, public or private, anywhere in North America. A cavalier attitude towards this reality may be the best source of encouragement we can give to those who prey on the young lives on our public schools. First and foremost, we must make our schools physically and psychologically safe for our students.

Towards a Solution

Many educators in North America are hard at work trying to improve public education, but they need help. If schools are to change, society has to change, and it cannot be the sole responsibilty of public schooling to change the direction of society. The effects of working in increasingly more violent environments have been the cause of much teacher burnout (Roper, 1998). Shamon (1996) notes that for teachers who remain in the profession the most important thing they can do to improve the image of public schooling is to remind the public that they are doing their best to fulfil the mandate of educating the nation's young. Teachers need to increase the momentum for innovating ideas and programs and publicize these so that people will be more aware of the importance of public education. These efforts will cost money. Then, as if that were not enough, the public needs to realize that if privatization of schools continues to syphon off needed funds, it will take years to bring schools up to the level of financing and status of reputation which they deserve.

Settings in which teachers are trying to educate children with aggressive and violent tendencies are often inadequately equipped and teachers do not have the specialized training necessary to deal with these challenges. Today more students with low attachment to school, poor academic performance, low social competence and attitudes in favor of breaking the law are attending public schools. Non-public schools tend to enroll students who do not have these problems for the very reason that their parents send them there. Causes for these behaviors are legion, and may possibly be attributed to unsatisfactory family environment and/or family relationships characterized by poor parenting skills, lack of parental supervision, insufficient nurturing and presocial bonding, ineffective or harsh discipline, or repeated exposure to situations of violence. Social inequities such as ethnic/racial discrimination or economic/demographic shifts that hamper adults' abilities to be gainfully employed may also be related causes (Huff and Trump, 1996).

Some critics suggest that what is missing in school is the will to learn; many students today have never experienced the satisfaction, the sheer exhilaration of achieving a goal through sustained effort. According to Bontempo (1995) for many young Americans "work" is a four letter word. Too much the modern generation has reaped the benefits of "instant everything" without exerting too much personal effort. It is doubtful that the school can by itself resolve all of the related frustrating maladies, but educators are making serious efforts to do just that. They need help.

Hwang (1995) contributes the cause of violence and lack of appreciation for work to four factors: poor academic attitudes, learning environment at home, lack of self-responsibility, and false self-esteem. Hwang blames American society for glamorizing easy success and the fast life. Current cultural fashion dictates that American children readily challenge authority and disdain intellectual development and achievement. As a result foreign born children of immigrant parents who have more traditional values, do better in school. The longer foreign-born students remain in American, the more academically indifferent they become. Hwang goes on to point out that student apathy can directly be linked to parental apathy, and contends that at no time in American history has the family become so fragmented. Parents are so busy socializing, working, feeding their addictions and searching for personal fulfillment, they have no time to spend on their children's education.

The problem is not the schools and not youth; the problem is parents and society. Youth are taught from the time of early childhood, directly or indirectly, that they have need to take little or no responsibility for behavioral outcomes. If something does not work out, the "system" is to blame. If a student fails, society is at fault, poverty is at fault, or teachers are at fault. Above all, our youth are being taught never to take responsibility for their own inaction or error. Coupled with this attitude, Hwang charges that American students have a false self-esteem; they are taught to feel good about themselves even if they have never accomplished anything, or done something of value for others or for society. Children are told that they are wonderful even when they indulge their energies primarily in self-gratification. As a result

American students are content with minimal achievements for which they expect to be awarded inflated approvals and undeserved grades so they can feel good about their "accomplishments" and about themselves. Then, when everything is said and done, critics expect the public school to fix things up.

But still there is hope. Educators are trying to meet these challenges by continuing to teach and by initiating new programs that might alleviate the situation and enhance learning. In terms of working to reduce violence, many new efforts in anger management and conflict resolution have been designed by caring teachers (Roper, 1998). Teachers can now receive training to learn preventative skills and strategies, and institutions that specialize in teacher education have a responsibility to provide it (Chetkow-Yanoov, 1996). Teachers will need to have a knowledge base about violence and learn methods of prevention. The strategies they will need to learn must include: (i) understanding and improving school climate; (ii) mastering skills of nonviolent conflict resolution; (iii) combatting factors that breed violent behavior; (iv) teaching impulse control; (v) giving students opportunity to practice problem solving; (vi) learning methods that reduce violence; and, (vii) knowing how to build authentic student self-esteem (White and Beal, 1999).

There is more good news. Not only have public school teachers shown that they have the motivation to tackle the problems that exits in our schools, they have demonstrated that they are capable of acquiring both the knowledge and skills to do so. An experiment on global education by Hasan (2000) in Jordan showed that teachers who participated in a program on the topic were willing to rethink their teaching role and the beliefs, conceptions and theories-in-use that support it. Many participants also shifted their behavior to be more in harmony with the expected role, particularly when they had administrative support. Developing teacher skills in global education was even more successful. Hasan argues that global education, perhaps more than any other topic, can induce positive changes in teachers' beliefs and conceptions, enrich their professional skills and strategies, and enhance their self-efficacy. But it is necessary to give credit where credit is due. Public school teachers have shown their commitment to positive change in our schools but they cannot singly induce societal reform all by themselves. Thus the question arises; "Can teachers expect a little help from people in the various societal sectors who must also take at least a little blame for the educational malaise within which we find ourselves?"

Where to Now?

The model adopted by the Edmonton Public School Board will not be followed by many school districts, but it merits further attention. It is a system that incorporates more alternatives than any other system in North

America. If the concern for parental choice in education is the issue, Edmonton's arrangement is worth examining. Choice, per se, however, is not the primary concern with public schools; safe, quality education is. The best way to accomplish this is to put as much money, energy and effort into the enterprise as we would if we really believed in it. Imagine the results!

Public schools are not in need of repair; they are not in need of criticism; they do not need to be dismantled. They are simply in need of support.

References

Abraham, Willard. (1964). *A Time for Teaching*. New York, NY: Harper & Row.

Adams, Don. (1972). *Schooling and Social Change in Modern America*. New York, NY: David McKay.

Addams, Jane. (1990). *Twenty Years and Hull-House: With Autobiographical Notes*. Chicago, IL: University of Chicago Press.

Adler, Mortimer. (1940). *How to Read a Book*. New York, NY: Simon and Schuster.

Adler, Mortimer J. (1942). In Defence of the Philosophy of Education. *The Forty-First Yearbook of the National Society for the Study of Education, Part I: Philosophy of Education*. Nelson B. Henry, ed. Chicago, IL: University of Chicago Press, pp. 197-250.

Adler, Mortimer J. (1964). The Future of Democracy: A Swan Song. *Humanistic Education and Western Civilization*. Arthur A. Cohen, ed. New York, NY: Holt, Rinehart and Company, pp. 30-43.

Adler, Mortimer J., and Peter Wolff. (1959). *A General Introduction to the Great Books and to a Liberal Education*. Chicago, IL: Encyclopedia Britannica.

Apple, Michael W. (2000). The Cultural Politics of Home Schooling. *Peabody Journal of Education, 75(1 & 2)*, pp. 256-271.

Archambault, Reginald D., ed. (1964). *John Dewey on Education: Selected Writings*. New York, NY: Modern Library.

Arnott, Kim. (Spring, 1997). *Home and School. Education Today, 9(2)*, pp. 16-21.

Arons, S. (1983). *Compelling Belief: The Culture of American Schooling*. Amherst, MA: University of MA Press.

Asano, Makoto. (Spring, 2000). School Reform, Human Rights, and Global Education. *Theory Into Practice, 39(2)*, pp. 104-110.

Audet, Louis-Phillipe. (1970a). Attempts to Develop a School System for Lower Canada. *Canadian Education: A History*. J. Donald Wilson, Robert Stamp and Louis-Phillipe Audet, eds. Scarborough, ON: Prentice-Hall, pp. 145-166.

Audet, Louis-Phillipe. (1970b). Education in Canada East and Quebec: 1840-1875. *Canadian Education: A History*. J. Donald Wilson, Robert Stamp and Louis-Phillipe Audet, eds. Scarborough, ON: Prentice-Hall, pp. 166-189.

Baines, Lawrence, Chris Muire and Gregory Stanley. (Winter, 1999). The Public School as Wasteland. *Contemporary Education, LXX(2)*, pp. 18-24.

Baldwin, Robert E. (July, 1982). Freedom of Choice in Education. *American Education, 19(6)*, pp. 17-23.

Barman, J. (1984). *Growing up British in British Columbia: Boys in Private School.* Vancouver, BC: University of British Columbia.

Baruth, Leroy, and M. Lee Manning. (1992). *Multicultural Education of Children and Adolescents.* Needham Heights, MA: Allyn and Bacon.

Bayles, Ernest E., and Bruce L. Hood. (1966). *Growth of American Educational Thought and Practice.* New York, NY: Harper & Row.

Beck, Clive. (1990). *Better Schools: A Values Perspective.* New York, NY: The Falmer Press.

Becker, Henry J., Kathryn Nakagawa and Ronald G. Corwin. (Spring, 1997). *Teachers College Record, 98(3)*, pp. 511-536.

Bell, Daniel. (1973). *The Coming of the Post-Industrial Society.* New York NY: Basic Books.

Bennett, Christine I. (1990). *Comprehensive Multicultural Education: Theory and Practice. Second edition.* Boston, MA: Allyn and Bacon.

Benveniste, Luis A., and Patrick J. McEwan. (May, 2000). Constraints to Implementing Educational Innovations: The Case of Multigrade Schools. *International Review of Education, 46(1-2)*, pp. 31-48.

Bergen, John J. (December, 1982). The Private School Movement in Alberta. *Alberta Journal of Educational Research, XXVIII(4)*, pp. 315-336.

Bergen, John J. (1990). The Emergence and Expansion of Private Schools in Canada. *Canadian Public Education System: Issues and Prospects,* Y. L. Jack Lam, ed. Calgary, AB: Detselig Enterprises, pp. 3-30.

Bestor, Arthur. (1953). *Educational Wastelands.* Urbana, IL: The University of Illinois Press.

Bittner, Marie. (March, 1995). Must Schools Protect Students from Harm? *The High School Journal, 78(3)*, pp. 159-163.

Blaschke, Charles. (September, 1971). From Gold Stars to Green Stamps. *Nation's Schools, 88(3)*, pp. 51-52.

Bode, Boyd H. (1927). *Modern Educational Theories.* New York, NY: Macmillan Press.

Bontempo, Barbara. (Summer, 1995). The Will to Learn. *Education, 115(4)*, pp. 491-492.

Bosetti, Lynn. (Summer, 2000). Alberta's Charter Schools: Paradox and Promises. *Alberta Journal of Educational Research, XLVI(2)*, pp. 179-190.

Boulding, Kenneth E. (1975). Predictive Reliability and the Future: The Need for Uncertainty. *The Future of Education: Perspectives on Tomorrow's Schooling.* Louis Rubin, ed. Boston, MA: Allyn and Bacon, pp. 57-74.

Bowers, C. A. (1969). *The Progressive Educator and the Depression: The Radical Years.* New York, NY: Random House.

Bowers, C A. (1974). *Cultural Literacy for Freedom.* Eugene, OR: Elan Publishers.

Brameld, Theodore. (1965). *Education as Power.* New York, NY: Holt, Rinehart and Winston.

Bremer, John and Michael von Moschzisker. (1971). *The School Without Walls: Philadelphia's Parkway Program.* New York, NY: Holt, Rinehart, and Winston.

Breneman, David W. (1983). Where Would Tuition Tax Credits Take Us? Should We Agree to Go? *Public Dollars for Private Schools: The Case for Tuition Tax Credits.* Thomas James and Henry M. Levin, eds. Philadelphia, PA: Temple University Press, pp. 115-129.

Brown, Frank. (February, 1995). Privatization of Public Education. *Education and Urban Society, 27(2)*, pp. 114-126.

Brubacher, John S. (1966). *A History of the Problems of Education.* New York, NY: McGraw-Hill Book Co.

Bruner, Jerome.S. (1963). *The Process of Education.* New York, NY: Vintage Books.

Bruner, Jerome S. (1966). *Toward a Theory of Instruction.* Cambridge, MA: Belknap Press.

Burrup, Percy E. (1960). *The Teacher and the Public School System.* New York, NY: Harper & Row.

Buski, Julius. (Fall, 1995). Charter Schools – Not the Answer! *The ATA Magazine, 76(1)*, pp. 30, 32.

Butler, R. W. (1995). Home Schooling: An Effective Environment for Programmed Instruction. *Home School Researcher, 11(4)*, pp. 7-16.

Butts, R. Freeman. (September, 1979). Educational Vouchers: The Private Pursuit of the Public Purse. *Phi Delta Kappan, 60*: pp. 7-8.

Carl, Jim. (Winter, 1996). Unusual Allies: Elite and Grass-roots Origins of Parental Choice in Milwaukee. *Teachers College Record, 98(2)*, pp. 266-285.

Catterall, James S., and Henry M. Levin. (April/July, 1982). Public and Private Schools: Evidence on Tuition Tax Credits. *Sociology of Education, 55*: pp. 144-151.

Cheal, John E., Harold C. Melsness and Arthur W. Reeves. (1962). *Educational Administration: The Role of the Teacher.* Toronto, ON: the Macmillan Company.

Chetkow-Yanoov, Benyamin. (1996). Conflict-Resolution Can Be Taught. *Peabody Journal of Education, 71(3)*, pp. 12-28.

Cohen, J. M. and M. J. Cohen. (1960). *Dictionary of Quotations.* Markham, ON: Penguin Books.

Coleman, James S. (January/February, 1982). Public Schools, Private Schools and the Public. *American Education,* pp. 17-22.

Coleman, James S., E. A. Campbell, C. J. Hobson, J. McPartland, A. M. Mood, F. D. Weinfeld, and R. L. York (1966). *Equality of Opportunity.* Washington, DC: National Center for Educational Statistics, US Government Printing Office.

Conant, James B. (1959). *The American High School Today: A First Report to Interested Citizens.* New York, NY: McGraw-Hill.

Contreras, A. Reynalso. (February, 1995). The Charter School Movement in California and Elsewhere. *Education and Urban Society, 27(2)*, pp. 213-228.

Coombs, Philip H. (1968). *The World Educational Crisis: A Systems Analysis.* New York, NY: Oxford University Press.

Coons, John E. (September, 1979). Of Family Choice and Public Education. *Phi Delta Kappan, 60*: pp. 10-13.

Coontz, S. (1992). *The Way We Never Were: American Families and the Nostalgia Trap.* New York: Basic Books.

Cooper, Bruce S. (1988). *The Changing Universe of US Private Schools. Comparing Public and Private Schools: Volume I: Institutions and Organizations.* Thomas James and Henry M. Levin, eds. London, UK: The Palmer Press, pp. 18-45.

Counts, George S. (1963). *Dare the School Build a New Social Order? The Teacher and the Taught.* Ronald Gross, ed. New York, NY: Dell.

Cox, Donald W., and Liza Lazorki. (1972). *A School Without Walls: A City for a Classroom. Education in a Dynamic Society: A Contemporary Sourcebook.* Dorothy Westby-Gibson, ed. Reading, MS: Addison-Wesley. pp. 273-277.

Crain, Robert L., and Christine H. Rossell. (1989). Catholic Schools and Racial Segregation. *Public Values, Private School.* Neal E. Devins, ed. London, UK: The Falmer Press, pp. 184-214.

Cremin, Lawrence A. (1961). *The Transformation of the School.* New York, NY: Random House.

Culkin, John M., S.J. (1970). John M. Culkin. *Summerhill: For and Against.* New York, NY: Hart Publishing Company, pp. 26-33.

Darling, John, Christopher Hammond, and Sheila Nataraj Kirby. (1988). *Public Versus Private Choice: The Case of Minnesota. Comparing Public and Private Schools: Volume I: Institutions and Organizations.* Thomas James and Henry M. Levin, eds. London, UK: The Falmer Press, pp. 243-267.

Darling, John. (Spring, 1994). Summerhill: From Neill to the Nineties. *The Educational Forum, 58(3)*, pp. 244-251.

Dembo, Myron H., and Donald A. Wilson. (May, 1973). A Performance Contracting in Speed Reading. *Journal of Reading, 16*: pp. 627-633.

Dewey, John. (1964). The Relation of Science and Philosophy as a Basis for Education. *John Dewey on Education: Selected Writings.* Reginald D. Archambault, ed. New York, NY: Modern Library, pp. 15-22.

Dickinson, William. (1971). *Performance Contracting: A Guide for School Board Members and Community Leaders.* Evanston, IL: National School Board Association.

Dimitriadis, Greg, and Cameron McCarthy. (Winter, 1999). Violence in Theory and Practice: Popular Culture, Schooling, and the Boundaries of Pedagogy. *Educational Theory, 49(1),* pp. 125-138.

Dobson, Linda. (1998). *The Home Schooling Book of Answers.* Ricklin, CA: Prima Publishing.

Donovan, David L. (January, 1983). Schools Do Make a Difference. *Education Digest,* pp. 28-29.

Doyle, Dennis. (October, 1982). A Den of Inequity: Private Schools Reconsidered. *American Education,* pp. 11-18.

Edmonds, Ronald R., and John R. Fredericksen. (1979). *Search for Effective Schools: The Identification and Analysis of City Schools that are Instruction-Effective for Poor Children.* Cambridge, MA: Center for Urban Studies, Harvard University.

Egerton, John. (March, 1982). Can We Save the Schools? *The Progressive,* pp. 26-28.

Ehlers, Henry, ed. (1973). *Crucial Issues in Education.* Fifth edition. New York: Holt, Rinehart and Winston.

Elias, John L. (1975). A Critique of Paulo Freire's Revolutionary Theory. *Cutting Edge, 6(3),* pp. 12-21.

Elliott, Jean Leonard, and Augie Fleras. (1992). *Unequal Relations: An Introduction to Race and Ethnic Dynamics in Canada.* Scarborough, ON: Prentice-Hall Canada.

Elster, Charles, Patricia Linehan, Penny Weiss, and Carole Zangari. (Spring, 1994). Building (the) New Community School. *The Educational Forum, 58(3),* pp. 290-298.

Erickson, Donald A. (September, 1979). Should All the Nation's Schools Compete for Clients and Support? *Phi Delta Kappan, 60:* pp. 14-17, 77.

Evans, Evelyn P., Maria E. Stallions, Fred Damianos, and B. J. Orfely. (Fall, 1999). Charter Schools: Educational Evolution or Revolution? *The Educational Forum, 64(1),* pp. 20-24.

Fain, Stephen M., Robert Shostak and John F. Dean. (1979). *Teaching in America.* Dallas, TX: Scott, Foresman and Co.

Ferge, Susan. (1974). How Teachers Perceive the Relation Between School and Society. *Sociology of Education, 45(1),* pp. 1-22.

Finn, Chester E. (May and June, 1982). Public Support for Private Education, Part I and II, *American Education,* pp. 4-9.

Fleras, Augie and Jean Leonard Elliott. (1992). *The Challenge of Diversity: Multiculturalism in Canada.* Scarborough, ON: Nelson Canada.

Foy, Rena, ed. (1968). *The World of Education: Selected Readings.* New York: The Macmillan Co.

Frasier, James E. (1965). *An Introduction to the Study of Education.* Third Edition. New York: Harper & Ros.

Friesen, Bruce K., and John W. Friesen. (1996). *Perceptions of the Amish Way.* Dubuque, IA: Kendall/Hunt.

Friesen, John W. (1983). *Schools With A Purpose.* Calgary, AB: Detselig Enterprises.

Friesen, John W. (1993a). Formal Schooling Among the Ancient Ones: The Mystique of the Kiva. *American Indian Culure and Research Journal, 17:(4)*, pp. 55-68.

Friesen, John W. (1993b). *When Cultures Clash: Case Studies in Multiculturalism. Second edition.* Calgary, AB: Detselig Enterprises.

Friesen, John W. (1997). *Rediscovering the First Nations of Canada.* Calgary, AB: Detselig Enterprises.

Friesen, John W. (1998). They Still Believe in Values: An Analysis of Amish Elementary School Curriculum. *Multicultural Education Journal, 16(1)*, pp. 6-22.

Friesen, John W. (2000). *Do Christians Forgive? Well, Some Do . . .* Ottawa, ON: Borealis Press.

Friesen, Virginia Lyons. (2001). Home Schooled Adults and Their Values: A Comparative Exploratory Study. Unpublished Doctoral Dissertation. Calgary, AB: University of Calgary.

Froese-Germain, Bernie. (Fall/Automne, 1998). What We Know About School Choice. *Education Canada, 38(3)*, pp. 22-27.

Gagné, Antoinette. (September, 1996). Success at Contact: The Argument for Alternative Schools for At-Risk Youth. *The Alberta Journal of Educational Research, XLII(3)*, pp. 306-324.

Galardi, Robert. (Spring, 1994). Community High School – An Alternative. *The Educational Forum, 58(3)*, pp. 299-305.

Gamage, David T. (Summer, 1996). An Australian Alternative to Create More Effective Schools. *The Educational Forum, 60(4)*, pp. 361-368.

Garcia, Eugene. (1994). *Understanding and Meeting the Challenge of Student Cultural Diversity.* Boston, MA: Houghton-Mifflin.

Gay, Geneva. (April, 1983). Multiethnic Education: Historical Development and Future Prospects. *Phi Delta Kappan, 64*: pp. 560-561.

Gay, Geneva. (1992). Multicultural Education in the United States. *Beyond Multicultural Education: International Perspectives.* Kogila A. Moodley, ed. Calgary, AB: Detselig Enterprises, pp. 41-66.

Ghosh, Ratna. (1996). *Redefining Multicultural Education.* Toronto, ON: Harcourt Brace & Company.

Ghosh, Ratna, and Douglas Ray. (1987). *Social Change and Education in Canada.* Toronto, ON: Harcourt Brace Jovanovich Canada.

Gibson, Margaret. (1976). Approaches to Multicultural Education in the US: Some Concepts and Assumptions. *Anthropology and Education Quarterly, 7(4)*, pp. 7-18.

Gilbert, Robert N. and Mike Robins. (1998). *Welcome to Our World: Realities of High School Students.* Thousand Oaks, CA: Corwin Press.

Giles, T. E. and A. J. Proudfoot. (1984). *Educational Administration in Canada. Third edition.* Calgary, AB: Detselig Enterprises.

Glasser, William. (1969) *Schools Without Failure.* New York, NY: Harper & Row.

Glatthorn, Allan A. (1975). *Alternatives in Education: Schools and Programs.* New York, NY: Dodd, Mead & Co.

Gollnick, Donna M., and Philip C. Chinn. (1986). *Multicultural Education in a Pluralistic Society. Second edition.* Columbus, OH: Charles E. Merrill.

Goodlad, John I. (1983). *A Place Called School.* New York, NY: McGraw-Hill.

Goodlad, John I., and Robert H. Anderson. (1963). *The Nongraded Elementary School. Revised edition.* New York, NY: Harcourt, Brace & World.

Gorder, Cheryl. (1996). *Home Schools: An Alternative.* Mesa, AZ: Blue Bird.

Gordon, Milton. (1964). *Assimilation in American Life: The Role of Race, Religion and National Origins.* New York, NY: Oxford University Press.

Gosden, P. H. J. H. (1969). *How They Were Taught: An Anthology of Contemporary Accounts of Learning and Teaching in England, 1800-1950.* Oxford, UK: Basil Blackwell.

Gossage, C. (1977). *A Question of Privilege: Canada's Independent Schools.* Toronto, ON: Peter Martin Associates Ltd.

Grant, Carl A., ed. (1995). *Educating for Diversity: An Anthology of Multicultural Voices.* Needham Heights, MA: Allyn and Bacon.

Grant, Carl A., and Susan Millar. (1992). Research and Multicultural Education: Barriers, Needs and Boundaries. *Beyond Multicultural Education: International Perspectives.* Kogila A. Moodley, ed. Calgary, AB: Detselig Enterprises, pp. 201-214.

Griffith, M. (1997). *The Home Schooling Handbook: From Preschool to High School, A Parents' Guide.* Rocklin, CA: Prima Publishing.

Gross, Richard E. (1962). *Heritage of American Education.* Boston, MA: Allyn and Bacon.

Gue, Leslie R. (1985). *An Introduction to Educational Administration in Canada. Second edition.* Toronto, ON: McGraw-Hill.

Guterson, D. (1992). *Family Matters: Why Home Schooling Makes Sense.* San Diego, CA: Harcourt Brace & Company.

Guppy, Neil, and Scott Davies. (Summer, 1999). Understanding Canadians' Declining Confidence in Public Education. *Canadian Journal of Education, 24(3)*, pp. 265-280.

Haché, Denis. (Spring, 1999). Public Education at the Dawn of the New Millennium: The New Zealand Experiment. *McGill Journal of Education, 34(2)*, pp. 113-134.

Harris, Gregg. (1988). How Does Home Schooling Help Society? *Schooling Choices: An Examination of Private, Public and Home Education,* H. Wayne House, ed. Portland, OR: Multnomah, pp. 231-239.

Harris III, J. John and Richard E. Fields. (Fall, 1982). Outlaw Generation: A Legal Analysis of the Home Instruction Movement. *Educational Horizons, 61:* pp. 26-31.

Hasan, El-Sheikh. (Spring, 2000). Improving the Quality of Learning: Global Education as a Vehicle for School Reform. *Theory Into Practice, 39(2)*, pp. 97-103.

Hawkins, Jr., Robert B. (October, 1982). Tuition Tax Credits: Another Voice. *American Education, 18:8,* pp. 9-10.

Henchley, Norman. (1988). Quality in Canadian Public Education: Some Future Perspectives. *Quality in Canadian Public Education: A Critical Assessment.* Hugh A. Stephenson and J. Donald Wilson, eds. London, UK: The Falmer Press, pp. 135-152.

Hendry, Graham D. (April, 1996). Constructivism and Educational Practice. *Australian Journal of Education, 40(1),* pp. 19-45.

Hill, Paul T. (2000). Home Schooling and the Future of Public Education. *Peabody Journal of Education, 75(1 & 2),* pp. 20-31.

Hirsch, Jr., E. D. (1996). *The Schools We Need and Why We Don't Have Them.* New York, NY: Doubleday.

Holt, John. (1964). *How Children Fail.* New York, NY: Pitman.

Holt, John. (1973). How Children Fail. *Analyses of Contemporary Education.* Allan C. Ornstein and W. Eugene Hedley, eds. New York, NY: Thomas Crowell, pp. 50-82.

Holt, John. (February, 1983). Schools and Home Schoolers: A Fruitful Partnership. *Phi Delta Kappan, 64:* pp. 391-394.

House, Ernest R. (1992). Multicultural Education in Canada and the United States. *The Canadian Journal of Program Evaluation, 7:1,* pp. 133-156.

House, H. Wayne, ed. (1988). *Schooling Choices: An Examination of Private, Public & Home Education.* Portland, OR: Multnomah.

Huff, C. Ronald, and Kenneth S. Trump. (August, 1996). School Safety Initiatives in Urban and Suburban School Districts. *Education and Urban Society, 28(4),* pp. 396-411.

Hunter, Brenda. (1991). *Home by Choice: Creating Emotional Security in Children.* Portland, OR: Multnomah.

Hutchins, Robert M. (1943). *Education for Freedom.* Baton Rouge, LA: Louisiana State University Press.

Hutchins, Robert. (1953). *The Conflict in Education.* New York, NY: Harper and Row.

Hwang, Yong G. (Summer, 1995). Student Apathy. Lack of Self-Responsibility and False Self-Esteem are Failing American Schools. *Education, 15(4),* pp. 484-490.

Ignas, Edward. (1981). *The Traditional American Educational System, Comparative Educational Systems.* Edward Ignas and Raymond J. Corsini, eds. Itasca, IL: F. E. Peacock Publishers, pp. 1-44.

Illich, Ivan, and Dennis Sullivan. (1974). Roads and Highways, Learning and Schools: Alternatives in Education. *Controversies in Education.* Dwight W. Allen and Jeffrey C. Hecht, eds. Philadelphia, PA: W. B. Saunders Co., pp. 12-18.

Jackson, Philip W., Amitai Etzioni, and John Ohlinger. (1973). *A Farewell o Schools – No! Crucial Issues in Education.* Fifth edition. Henry Ehlers, ed. New York, NY: Holt, Rinehart and Winston, pp. 207-213.

Jobling, J. K. (1974). Jean-Baptiste Meilleur: Architect of Lower Canada's School System. *Profiles of Canadian Educators.* Robert S. Patterson, John W. Chalmers and John W. Friesen, eds. Toronto, ON: D. C. Heath, pp. 100-117.

Johnson, Christopher. (February/March, 1982). The Future of Canadian Education. *Today's Education,* pp. 14-17.

Johnson, David W., and Roger T. Johnson. (1975). *Learning Together and Alone: Cooperation, Competition, and Individualization.* Englewood Cliffs, NJ: Prentice-Hall.

Johnson, David W., and Roger T. Johnson. (1985). Cooperative Learning and Adaptive Education. *Adapting Instruction to Individual Differences.* Margaret C. Wang and Herbert J. Walberg, ed. Berkeley, CA: McCutchan Publishing Co., pp. 105-134.

Johnson, David W., and Roger T. Johnson. (April, 1996). Reducing School Violence Through Conflict Resolution Training. *NASSP Bulletin, 80*(579), pp. 11-18.

Johnson, F. Henry. (1968). *A Brief History of Canadian Education.* Toronto, ON: McGraw-Hill.

Johnson, Tony W. (May, 1982). Educational Vouchers: An Idea Whose Time Has Come. *USA Today,* pp. 16-19.

Kahlenberg, Richard D. (December, 2000). Mixing Classes: Why Economic Desegregation Hold the Key to School Reform. *The Washington Monthly, 32*(12), pp. 9-14.

Kallin, Horace Meyer. (1924). *Culture and Democracy in the United States.* New York, NY: Boni and Liveright.

Kanpol, Barry. (1992). Postmodernism in Education Revisited: Similarities Within Differences and the Democratic Imaginary. *Educational Theory, 42*(2), pp. 217-229.

Kerr, Donna H. (1976). *Educational Policy: Analysis, Structure and Justification.* New York, NY: David McKay and Co.

Klages, Mary. (1997). Postmodernism. Online, English 1010 Home Page.

Klicka, Christopher J. (1993). *The Right Choice: Home Schooling.* Gresham, OR: Noble.

Koerner, James. (1963). *The Miseducation of American Teachers.* Boston, MA: Houghton-Mifflin.

Komisar, B. Paul. (Fall, 1992). Should We Push the Button? *Educational Horizons, 71*(1), pp. 18-22.

Kwong, Julia. (August, 1997). The Reemergence of Private Schools in China. *Comparative Education Review, 41*(3), pp. 244-259.

Laska, John A. (1976). *Schooling and Education: Basic Concepts and Problems.* New York, NY: D. Van Nostrand Co.

Lassinger, Leon M. (June/July, 1971). *Input. Instructor, 80*: pp. 19-20.

Lee, Valerie, Todd K., Chow-Hoy, David K. Burkam, Douglas Geverdt, and Becky A. Smerdon. (October, 1998). Sector Differences in High School Course Taking: A Private or Catholic School Effect? *Sociology of Education, 71*(4), pp. 314-334.

Leonard, George B. (1968). *Education and Ecstasy.* New York, NY: Dell.

Lieberman, Myron. (1960). *The Future of Public Education.* Chicago, IL: The University of Chicago Press.

Levin, Henry M. (1989) Education as a Public and Private Good. *Public Values, Private Schools.* Neal E. Devins, ed. London, UK: The Falmer Press, pp. 215-234.

Lin, Jing. (December, 1994). The Development and Prospect of Private Schools in China: A Preliminary Study. *Canadian and International Education, 23*(2), pp. 85-97.

Lines, P. (1991). Home Instruction: The Size and Growth of Movement. *Home Schooling: Political, Historical, and Pedagogical Perspectives.* Norwood, NJ: Ablex Publishing Corporation.

Livingstone, D. W., and D. J. Hart. (1987). The People Speak: Public Attitudes Toward Schooling in Canada. *Social Change and Education in Canada.* Ratna Ghosh and Douglas Ray, eds. Toronto: ON: Harcourt Brace Janovich Canada, pp. 3-27.

Lubienski, Chris. (2000). Wither the Common Good? A Critique of Home Schooling. *Peabody Journal of Education, 75(1 & 2),* pp. 207-232.

Lucas, Christopher J. (1984). *Foundations of Education: Schooling and the Social Order.* Englewood Cliffs, NJ: Prentice-Hall.

Lupul, Manoly R. (1970). Educational Crisis in the New Dominion to 1917. *Canadian Education: A History.* J. Donald Wilson, Robert Stamp and Louis-Phillipe Audet, eds. Scarborough, ON: Prentice-Hall, pp. 266-289.

Lyons, James E. (February, 1995). Contracting Out for Public School Support Services. *Education and Urban Society, 27*(2), pp. 154-167.

MacDonald, Irene M. (Summer/Fall, 1997). Violence in Schools: Multiple Realities. *The Alberta Journal of Educational Research, XLIII(3),* pp. 142-156.

MacEwan, Arthur. (Fall, 1996). Private School Enrollment: Some Numbers and Some Speculations. *Radical Teacher, No. 48,* pp. 6-11.

MacKinnon, Frank. (1962). *The Politics of Education.* Toronto, ON: University of Toronto Press.

Madaus, George F., Thomas Kellaghan, and Richard L. Schwab. (1989). *Teach Them Well: An Introduction to Education.* New York, NY: Harper & Row.

Madsen, Jean. (1996). *Private and Public School Partnerships: Sharing Lessons about Decentralization.* London, UK: The Falmer Press.

Mann, Horace. (1968). Means and Objects of Common School Education. *The World of Education: Selected Readings.* Rena Foy, ed. New York, NY: The Macmillan Co., pp. 19-23.

Manno, Bruno V., Chester E, Finn, jr., Louann A. Bierlein, and Gregg Vanourek. (Spring, 1998a). Charter Schools: Accomplishments and Dilemmas. *Teachers College Record, 99*(3), pp. 537-558.

Manno, Bruno V., Chester E, Finn, Jr., Louann A. Bierlein, and Gregg Vanourek. (Spring, 1998b). How Charter Schools Are Different: Lessons and Implications from a National Study. *Phi Delta Kappan, 79(7),* pp. 488-498.

Marchant, G., and S. C. MacDonald. (April, 1992). How Home Schoolers School: Ohio Profiles. San Francisco, CA: A paper presented at the Annual Meeting of the American Educational Research Association.

Maritain, Jacques. (1943). *Education at the Crossroads.* New Haven, CT: Yale University Press.

McClendon, Jonathan, ed. (1966). *Social Foundations of Education: Current Readings from the Behavioral Sciences.* New York, NY: The Macmillan Co.

McConville, J. Lawrence. (May, 1973). Evolution of Performance Contracting. *Educational Forum, 37(2),* pp. 443-452.

McDowell, Susan A., and Brian D. Ray. (2000). The Home Education Movement in Context, Practice, and Theory: Editors' Introduction. *Peabody Journal of Education, 75(1 & 2),* pp. 1-7.

McEwan, Patrick J., and Martin Carnoy. (Fall, 2000). The Effectiveness and Efficiency of Private Schools in Chile's Voucher System. *Educational Evaluation and Policy Analysis, 22(3),* pp. 213-240.

McGee, Clive. (Fall, 1995). The Development of a New National Curriculum in New Zealand. *The Educational Forum, 60(1),* pp. 56-63.

McGuckin, William. (1942). The Philosophy of Catholic Education. *The Forty-First Yearbook of the NSSE, Part I.* Nelson B. Henry, ed. Chicago, IL: University of Chicago Press, pp. 251-288.

McNeil, Jr., Jesse. (Spring, 1999). A University and Charter School Collaboration Born Out of Great Need. *Education, 119:3,* pp. 438-446.

McNeill, John L. (1974). Egerton Ryerson: Founder of Canadian (English-speaking) Education. *Profiles of Canadian Educators.* Robert S. Patterson, John W. Chalmers and John W. Friesen, eds. Toronto, ON: D. C. Heath, pp. 118-140.

McNergney, Robert F., Laurie A. Regelbrugge, and Jeffrey P. Harper. (1997). Multicultural Education in *Global Context. Research on the Education of Our Nation's Teachers, Teacher Education Yearbook V.* David M. Byrd and D. John McIntyre, eds. Thousand Oaks, CA: Corwin Press, pp. 7-25.

Mecklenburger, J. A. (January, 1972) Performance Contracting: One View. *Educational Leadership, 29:* pp. 297-300.

Mehl, Bernard. (1963). Education in American History. *Foundations of Education.* George F. Kneller, ed. New York: John Wiley and Sons, pp. 1-44.

Miller, Harry L., and Roger R. Woock. (1970). *Social Foundations of Urban Education.* Hinsdale, IL: Dryden Press.

Miller-Lachmann, Lynn, and Lorraine S. Taylor. (1995). *Schools for All: Educating Children in a Diverse Society.* Albany, NY, NY: Delmar Publishers.

Montagu, Ashley. (1958). *Education and Human Relations.* New York, NY: Grove Press.

Murphy, Joseph. (1990). The Educational Reform Movement of the 1980s: A Comprehensive Analysis. *The Educational Reform Movement of the 1980s: Perspectives and Cases.* Joseph Murphy, ed. Berkeley, CA: McCutchan Publishing Corp., pp. 3-56.

Musgrave, P. W. (1965). *The Sociology of Education.* London, ON: Methuen & Co.

Myers, Douglas. (1973). Where have All the Free Schools Gone? *The Failure of Educational Reform in Canada.* Douglas Myers, ed. Toronto, ON: McClelland and Stewart, pp. 75-94.

Myers, Charles B. and Douglas J. Simpson. (1998). *Re-Creating Schools: Places Where Everyone Learns and Likes It.* Thousand Oaks, CA: Corwin Press.

Nathan, Joe. (March, 1998). Heat and Light in the Charter School Movement. *Phi Delta Kappan, 79(7),* pp. 499-505.

Neatby, Hilda. (1953). *So Little for the Mind.* Toronto, ON: Clarke, Irwin.

Neill, A. S. (1960). *Summerhill: A Radical Approach to Child Rearing.* New York, NY: Hart Publishing Co.

Nelson, Fiona. (1973). Community Schools: A Sign of Hope. *The Failure of Educational Reform in Canada.* Douglas Myers, ed. Toronto, ON: McClelland and Stewart, pp. 119-133.

Netten, J. W. (1974). Edward Feild, Protagonist of Denominational Education. *Profiles of Canadian Educators.* Robert S. Patterson, John W. Chalmers and John W. Friesen, eds. Toronto, ON: D. C. Heath and Company, pp. 77-99.

Nikiforuk, Andrew. (November 15-21, 2000). Edmonton's Unorthodox Public School System Draws Attention. *Business Edge*, p. 11.

Oldenquist, Andrew. (1984). The Decline of American Education in the '60s and '70s. *Education 84/85.* Fred Schultz, ed. Guilford, CT: The Dushkin Publishing Group, pp. 90-95.

Ornstein, Allan C., and W. Eugene Hedley. (1973). *Analyses of Contemporary Education.* New York, NY: Thomas Crowell.

Ouellet, Fernand. (1992). Education in a Pluralist Society: Proposal for an Enrichment of Teacher Education. *Beyond Multicultural Education: International Perspectives.* Kogila A. Moodley, ed. Calgary, AB: Detselig Enterprises, pp. 281-302.

Palmer, Howard. (1982). *Patterns of Prejudice: A History of Nativism in Alberta.* Toronto, ON: McClelland and Stewart.

Parker, Franklin, and Betty J. Parker. (Spring, 1995). A Historical Perspective on School Reform. *The Educational Reform, 59(3)*, pp. 278-287.

Paterson, Francis R. A. (Winter, 2000). Teaching Intolerance: Anti-Catholic Bias in Voucher-Supported Schools. *The Educational Forum, 64(2),* pp. 139-149.

Patterson, Robert S. (1974). Hubert C. Newland, Theorist of Progressive Education. *Profiles of Canadian Educators.* Robert S. Patterson, John W. Chalmers and John W. Friesen, eds. Toronto, ON: D. C. Heath and Company, pp. 289-307.

Patrick, R. W. (1998). Public and Home School Collaboration in Alberta. Unpublished doctoral dissertation, Provo, UT: Brigham Young University.

Phillips, Charles E. (1955). *The Quance Lectures in Canadian Education.* Toronto, ON: Gage.

Phillips, D. C. (Summer, 2000). Interpreting the Seventies, or, Rashomon Meets *Educational Theory. Educational Theory, 50*(3), pp. 321-325.

Pincus, Fred L. (Fall, 1996). The Failure of School Privatization: Education Alternatives Inc. in Baltimore. *Radical Teacher, 48*: pp. 12-16.

Porter, John. (1987). *The Measure of Canadian Society: Education, Quality and Opportunity.* Ottawa, ON: Carleton University Press.

Postman, Neil. (1979a). *Teaching as a Subversive Activity.* New York, NY: Delacorte Press.

Postman, Neil. (1979b). *Teachings as a Conserving Activity.* New York, NY Delacorte Press.

Powell, Arthur G. (May, 1982). Appreciating the Dualism of Public and Private Schools. *Education Digest,* pp. 11-13.

Pratte, Richard. (1977). *Ideology & Education.* New York, NY: David McKay.

Priesnitz, W., and H. Priesnitz. (March, 1990). *Home-Based Education in Canada: An Investigation.* Unionville, ON: The Alternative Press.

Program Evaluation Section. (June, 1984). Ian Bazelgette Junior High School, Effective School Program, Calgary, AB: Calgary Board of Education, Office of the Chief Superintendent.

Proweller, Amira. (Summer, 1999). Shifting Identities in Private Education: Reconstructing Race at/in the Cultural Center. *Teachers College Record, 100(4)*, pp. 751-808.

Rafferty, Max. (1963). *What Are They Doing to Your Children?* New York, NY: The New American Library.

Rafferty, Max. (1970). What Are They Doing to Your Children? *Contemporary Critics of Education.* Howard Ozman, ed. Danville, IL: The Interstate Printers, pp. 163-170.

Raths, Louis E., M. Harmon, and Sidney B. Simon. (1978). *Values and Teaching: Second edition.* Columbus, OH: Charles E. Merrill Books.

Ravitch, Diane. (June, 1981). The Meaning of the New Coleman Report. *Phi Delta Kappan, 66*: pp. 718-720.

Ray, Brian D. (1994). *A Nationwide Study of Home Education in Canada: Family Characteristics, Student Achievement, and Other Topics.* Salem, OR: National Education Research Institute.

Ray, Brian D. (2000). Home Schooling: The Ameliorator of Negative Influences on Learning? *Peabody Journal of Education, 75(1 & 2),* pp. 71-106.

Reed, Martin. (May, 1972). Performance Contracting: Did We Learn Anything? *American School Board Journal, 159*: pp. 30-32.

Reimer, Everett. (1972). An Essay on Alternatives in Education. *The Radical Papers.* Harold W. Sobel and Arthur E. Saltz, eds. New York, NY: Harper and Row, pp. 154-179.

Resetar, M. A. (1990). An Exploratory Study of the Rationales Parents Have for Home Schooling. *Home Schooling Researcher, 6(2),* pp. 1-7.

Rettig, Marilies and Bill Hynd. (Fall, 2000). Education for All: Will It Ever Happen? *ATA Magazine, 80:4*, pp. 28-29.

Richey, Robert W. (1979). *Planning for Teaching: An Introduction to Education.* New York, NY: McGraw-Hill.

Rickover, H.G. (1960). *Education and Freedom.* New York, NY: E.P. Dutton.

Robert, Marc. (1976). *School Morale: The Human Dimension.* Niles, IL: Argus Communications.

Roper, Dale Ann D. (Summer, 1998). Facing Anger in Our Schools. *The Educational Forum, 52(4)*, pp. 363-368.

Rossi, Peter H., and Alice S. Rossi. (1968). Some Effects of Parochial School Education in America. *The Sociology of Education.* Robert R. Bell and Holger R. Stub, eds. Homewood, IL: The Dorsey Press, pp. 53-78.

Rubin, Louis. (1975). *The Future of Education: Perspectives on Tomorrow's Schooling.* Boston, MA: Allyn and Bacon.

Santo, Hubert. (September, 1980). Voucher Plan: A Private School Principal's Critique. *NASSP Bulletin, 64*: pp. 93-98.

Scanlon, Robert G. (1975). Policy and Planning for the Future. *The Future of Education: Perspectives on Tomorrow's Schooling.* Boston, MA: Allyn and Bacon, pp. 83-95.

Schnaiberg, L. (June, 1996). Staying Home From School. Education Week, Online, www.edweek.org.

Schofield, John. (2001). Saving Our Schools. *Maclean's. 114(20),* pp. 22-29.

Sefa Dei, George J., Irma Marcia James, Leeno Luke Karumanchery, Sonia James-Wilson, and Jasmin Zine. (2000). *Removing the Margins: The Challenges and Possibilities of Inclusive Schooling.* Toronto, ON: Canadian Scholars Press.

Shamon, Janice. (Fall, 1996). Massachusetts Charter Schools: When Reform Goes Wrong. *Radical Teacher, 48*: pp. 17-26.

Sheffer, S. (1992). At-Home Education. *Encyclopedia of Early Childhood Education.* Leslie R. Williams & Doris Pronin Fromberg, eds. New York: Garland, pp. 139-140.

Shellenberger, E. C. (1998). An Ethnographic Case Study of Three Home Schooling Families in Central Pennsylvania and Their Sociocultural Support Groups. CD-ROM, Abstract from ProQuest File: Dissertation Abstracts Item: 9836763.

Shields, Carolyn M., and Linda J. LaRocque. (Winter, 1998). Year-Round Schooling: A Catalyst for Pedagogical Change. *Alberta Journal of Educational Research, XLIV(4),* pp 366-382.

Sianjina, Rayton R. (Winter, 1999). Parental Choice, School Vouchers, and the Separation of Church and State: Legal Implications. *The Educational Forum, 63(2),* pp. 108-112.

Siccone, Frank. (1995). *Celebrating Diversity: Building Self-Esteem in Today's Multicultural Classrooms.* Boston, MA: Allyn and Bacon.

Silberman, Charles E. (1973). Crisis in the Classroom. *Analysis of Contemporary Education.* Allan C. Ornstein and W. Eugene Hedley, eds. New York: Thomas Crowell, pp. 292-317.

Simon, Sidney B, L. W. Howe and H. Kirschenbaum. (1972). *Values Clarification: A Handbook of Practical Strategies for Teachers and Students.* New York: Hart Publishing Company.

Soles, A. E. (1988). Surmounting the Insurmountable: Suggestions for Improving Canadian Public Education. *Canadian Public Education: A Critical Assessment.* Hugh A. Stevenson and J. Donald Wilson, eds. London, UK: The Falmer Press, pp. 119-133.

Spiro, Melford E. (1996). Postmodernist Anthropology, Subjectivity, and Science. *Comparative Studies in Society and History, V*: pp. 759-780.

Stamp, Robert M. (1975).*A bout Schools: What Every Canadian Parent Should Know.* Don Mills, ON: New Press.

Stinnett, T. M., and Albert J. Huggett. (1963). *Professional Problems of Teachers.* New York, NY: The Macmillan Company.

Sugarman, D. Stephen. (1980). Family Choice in Education. *Oxford Review of Education, 6(1),* pp. 31-40.

Tanner, Daniel. (March, 1973). Performance Contracting: Contrivance of the Industrial Government at Complex. *Intellect, 101*: pp. 361-365.

Taylor, Lesley Ann. (Spring, 1997). Home in School: Insights on Education Through the Lens of Home Schoolers. *Theory Into Practice, 36(2)*, pp. 110-116.

Tiedt, Pamela L., and Iris M. Tiedt. (1979). *Multicultural Teaching: A Handbook of Activities, Information and Resources.* Boston, MA: Allyn and Bacon.

Tirozzi, Gerald N. (December, 1999). Building a Movement for Community Schools. *NASSP Bulletin, 83(611),* pp. 1-7.

Toews, F. J., and D. M. Barker. (November, 1983). The Baz Attack: One School's Self-Improvement Program. *The ATA Magazine, 64(1),* pp. 12-23.

Tonsmeire, J. Kelly. (1977). Alternative Public Education: An Analysis. *Cutting Edge, 9(1)*, pp. 23-25.

Trump, Kenneth S. (1998). *Practical School Security: Basic Guidelines for Safe and Secure Schools.* Thousand Oaks, CA: Corwin Press.

Tyack, David and Elizabeth Hansot. (1984). Hard Times, Hard Choices: The Case for Coherence in Public School Leadership. *Education 84/85.* Fred Schultz, ed. Guilford, CT: The Dushkin Publishing Group, pp. 4-7.

Ulich, Robert. (1966). *Crisis and Hope in American Education.* New York, NY: Atherton Press.

Van Galen, Jane A. (1991). Ideologues and Pedagogues: Parents Who Teach Their Children at Home. *Home Schooling: Political, Historical, and Pedagogical Perspectives.* Jane Van Galen and Mary Anne Pitman, eds. Norwood, NJ: Ablex Publishing Corporation, pp. 63-76.

Wagner, Tony. (March, 1998). Change as Collaborative Inquiry: A Constructivist Methodology for Reinventing Schools. *Phi Delta Kappan, 79(7),* pp. 512-517.

Walford, Geoffrey. (1990). *Privatization and Privilege in Education.* London, UK: Routledge.

Warren, Donald. (1990). Passage of Rites: on the History of Educational Reform in the United States. *The Educational Reform Movement of the 1980s: Perspectives and Cases.* Joseph Murphy, ed. Berkeley, CA: McCutchan Publishing Corp., pp. 57-81.

Wees, W. R. (1967). The Way Ahead. Lectures delivered Under the Quance Lectures in Canadian Education. Toronto, ON: W. J. Gage.

Wees, W. R. (1971). *Nobody Can Teach Anyone Anything.* Toronto, ON: Doubleday.

Weinzweig, P. (1977). Socialization in Canadian Private Schools. *Education, Change and Society: A Sociology of Canadian Education.* Richard A. Carlton, Louise A. Colley and Neil J. MacKinnon, eds.Toronto, ON: Gage Publishing, pp. 351-358.

Wells, Amy Stuart, Alejandra Lopez, Janelle Scott, and Jennifer Jellison Holme. (Summer, 1999). Charter Schools as Postmodern Paradox: Rethinking

Social Stratification in an Age of Deregulated School Choice. *Harvard Educational Review, 69(2),* pp. 172-204.

White, Barbara L., and Gloria D. Beal. (Fall, 1999). Violence in Schools as Perceived by Preservice and In-service Teachers. *Contemporary Education, LXXI(1)*, pp. 31-38.

Whitty, Geoff, Sally Power, and David Halpin. (1998). *Devolution and Choice in Education: The School, The State and the Market.* Buckingham, UK: Open University Press.

Willie, Charles V. (Summer, 2000). The Evolution of Community Education: Content and Mission. *Harvard Educational Review, 70(2),* pp. 191-209.

Wilson, J. Donald. (1970). Education in Upper Canada: Sixty Years of Change. *Canadian Education: A History.* J. Donald Wilson, Robert M. Stamp, and Louis-Philippe Audet, eds. Scarborough, ON: Prentice-Hall of Canada, pp. 190-213.

Winchester, Ian. (April, 2,000). Some Challenges to Publicly Funded Education in the New Millennium. *Journal of Educational Thought, 34(1)*, pp. 1-9.

Witte, John F., and Christopher A. Thorn. (May, 1996). Who Chooses? Voucher and Interdistrict Choice Programs in Milwaukee. *American Journal of Education, 104(3)*, pp. 186-217.

Wotherspoon, Terry. (1998). *The Sociology of Education in Canada.* Toronto, ON: Oxford University Press.

Young, David G. (1981). *Educational Vouchers: Boon or Bane.* Edmonton, AB: Government of Alberta, Department of Educational Planning and Research.

Zeigler, Harmon and Wayne Peak. (1970). The Political Functions of the Educational System. *Sociology of Education, 43(2),* pp. 115-142.

Zentner, H. (1972). Accountability in a Permissive Society. *Educational Accountability.* T. E. Giles, ed. Calgary, AB: Alberta Council on School Administration, pp. 76-84.

Index

A Nation at Risk 23, 56
Aboriginal 17, 20, 147
Absolute truth and knowledge 66
Act of Union of 1841 28
Adler, Mortimer 35, 63, 64, 65, 67
Alberta 17, 25, 30, 31, 57, 71, 83, 84,
   92, 123, 127, 130, 131, 133, 135,
   139, 146, 151
Alternative Schools 40, 84, 88, 98, 99,
   100, 102, 103
Alternative High School 84
Aquinas, Thomas 66
Australia 17

Barnard, Henry 35
Baltimore 120
Behaviorism 74
Bestor, Arthur 61
Blank tablet mind 61
Bode, Boyd 22, 74, 76
Brameld, Theodore 70
British North America (BNA) Act of
   1867 25, 30, 82, 83, 97
Brown, Rap 46
Bruner, Jerome S. 22, 65, 66
Bush, President George 22, 92
Bush, President George W. 92

Callahan, Raymond 72
Canadian Constitution 97
Canadian Constitution Act of 1982 83
Canadian Education Association 33
Carleton, Frank Tracy 72
Carmichael, Stokely 46
Carter, President Jimmy 23
Charter of Rights 55
Charter Schools 11, 55, 57, 77, 84, 88,
   92, 93, 94, 103, 111, 131
   community schools in Ohio 131
   criticisms of 136
   defined 132, 133
   history 131

Charter Schools, Renaissance Charter
   School 137
Childs, John L. 69
Clinton, President Bill 22, 133
Coleman, James S. 85
Coleman Report 85, 90, 113
Common School Act of 1816 27
Common School Act of 1846 28
Common School Ordinance of 1869
   30
Community Alternative High School
   45
Community Schools 44
Compulsory school attendance 21
Conant Report 38, 39, 75
Conant, James B. 22, 75
Constitution of the United States 97
Constitutional Act of 1791 27
Constructivism 75, 76
Contact School 84
Cooperative Learning 49
Counts, George Sylvester 22, 69, 70
Cultural diversity in Canada 145
Cultural diversity in the United States
   144

Dewey, John 22, 31, 35, 36, 59, 60,
   61, 62, 64, 65, 68, 71, 72, 76, 77,
   99, 101
DeWolfe, Loren 31, 71
Diversity in schools 99

Economic Council of Canada 57
Edmonton, Alberta 17
Education Alternatives Incorporated
   120
Education for self-realization 42
Educational choice 23
Effective schools 51, 98
English grammar school 19
Existentialists 76
Experience-centred education 71

Franklin, Benjamin 21
Free Education 22
Free Schools 98

Gardner, John W. 75
Gestalt 76
Goodlad, John 39, 40
Goodman, Paul 39
Grammar School Act of 1807 27
Grant, President Ulysses S. 81
Great Books 63, 64
Great Panacea, The 72

Hall, G. Stanley 36
Heidegger, Martin 74
Holistic (wholistic) teaching 67, 81
Holt, John 125
Home schooling 11, 56, 57, 84, 103,
    123, 153
Home schooling, reasons to 123, 125
Home schooling, values 126
Hughes, Archbishop John 81
Hughes, James L. 71, 72
Hutchins, Robert Maynard 35, 63,
    64, 65, 67

Illich, Ivan 39
Industrial(ism) Revolution 71, 72, 76

James, William 76

Kierkegarrde, Soren 74
Kilpatrick, William Heard 22, 36,
    69, 70
Koerner, James 61
Kozol, Jonathan 39

Latin grammar schools 21
Laurier-Greenway Agreement 30
Leiberman, Myron 38, 39
Leonard, George 39
Locke, John 61
Logos 84

Madras Schools 29
Mann, Horace 14, 21, 35

Manual training 71
Maritain, Jacques 66
Massachusettes 20, 21, 106, 138, 139
McGuckin, Thomas 67
Meilleur, Jean-Baptiste 26
Minnesota 57, 112, 131, 132
Montagu, Ashley 39
Montessori, Maria 100
Morrison, Henry Clinton 101
Morrison Plan 101

National Education Association 22, 38
Neatby, Hilda 61
Neill, A.S. 39, 41, 43, 88
Neitsche, Friedrich 74
NeoThomist 66, 67, 72
New Brunswick 25, 29
New Community School 45
Newfoundland school system 83
Newland, Hubert 31, 71
Nova Scotia 25, 29, 31, 71

Ontario Department of Education 71
Ontario 29, 54, 71, 84, 147, 151, 155
Open-area classroom 53

Packwood-Moynihan Tuition Tax
    Credit Bill 113
Parent advisory groups/councils 40
Parochial Schools 79, 80, 81, 82, 153
    funding 100
    Roman Catholic 81, 85
Peirce, Charles Sanders 76
Performance Contracting, defects 119
Performance Contracting defined 115
Pestalozzi, Johann Heinrich 76
Philadelphia Parkway Program 43
*Plains Indians Cultural Survival
    School* (PICSS) 84
Plato 64
Plymouth Colony 20
Postman, Neil 52
Postmodernism 76, 77
Pragmatic(tists) 36, 76
Principles of education 22

Private School versus Public School 93
Private Schools 11, 57, 79, 80, 89, 102,153
  advantages 93
  characteristics 79
  criticism of 86
  defending 85
  enrollment 92
  funding 100
  in China 90
  Packwood-Moynihan Tuition Tax Credit Bill 113
  parental choice for 91
  tax credit 112
Progressivism(ists) 38, 49, 60, 61, 62, 64, 65, 66, 67, 68, 69, 70, 71, 72, 73, 74, 75, 98, 100
Public Education, improving 157
Public Schooling
  versus Private 93
  need for 95
  origins 79, 81
  standards 63
  the future of 141
Puritans 20

Quebec 25, 28, 147

Rafferty, Max 61
Reagan, President Ronald 23, 92, 112
Reconstructionists 69, 70
Relativists 76
Renaissance Charter School, Texas 137
Rickover, Admiral Hyman 74, 75
Rugg, Harold 69, 101
Ryerson, Egerton 28

Sartre, Jean Paul 74, 76
School safety, myths 160
School Without Walls 43
Schools for excellence movement 56, 99
Seath, John 71

Silberman, Charles 39
Skinner, B.F. 36, 74
Smith-Hughes Act 72
Snedden, David 72
Social Frontier, The 70
Socialization 36, 48, 60, 69, 97, 116, 128, 129, 141
Spaulding, Frank 73, 74
Sputnik 38, 47, 74, 75
St. John's Boys Schools 88
Strachan, Bishop John 27
Summerhill 41, 43, 88
Sylvan Learning Systems 120
Syntopion 64

Tax credits, strengths and weaknesses 113
Tax credits for educational expenses 112
Tax-supported schools 21
Taylor, Fredrick W. 73
Teacher training 62
Texarcana 118, 119
Texas 137
Thorndike, Edward L. 36, 73, 74
Tranditionalsim(ists) 36, 60, 61, 62, 64, 65, 66, 75, 98

Unit Plan 101
United States Office of Education 33

Vietnam War 39, 42, 53, 120, 144
Violence in schools 16, 159
  cause 162
  preventative skills 163
Vocational education 71
Vocationalism 60, 61, 75
von Braun, Werner 74
Voucher (system) 27, 92, 103, 104, 114
Vouchers
  achievement model 106
  advantages 114
  Alum Rock Experiment 106
  California Family Choice Initiative 108

Vouchers
    California Family Choice Initiative
        108
    Coon-Sugarman Voucher Model
        105, 108
    Educational Voucher Agency 106
    Egalitarian Model 106
    Friedman's Unregulated Market
        Model 105
    Jencks Private Membership Model
        105, 106
    objection to 109
    Sizer-Whitten Model 105

War of Independence in 1776 79
Washburne, Carleton W. 101
Whitney's Industrial Education Act 71
Whole child 61, 102
Wholistic (holistic) education 67, 81
Winnetka Plan 101

Year-round School 120

MEMBER OF SCABRINI MEDIA

Québec, Canada
2001